Praise for *Becoming A Lea*

"Mike Easley was an active and excited learner in the executive development program at Grand Canyon University, and I admire his constant desire to be a better leader. Whether you are an individual just learning about self-leadership, a more experienced manager working on developing your skills as a team leader, or a seasoned servant leader at the executive level, *Becoming A Leader Worth Following* is the read. Mike's words are meaty and motivating as he speaks directly to you with leadership lessons from his own life and work— from Scout to CEO—that are real and relatable. This enjoyable book will leave you wanting more from Mike."

—Ken Blanchard, co-author of *The One Minute Manager*®
and *Simple Truths of Leadership*

"Mike has undertaken the difficult task of providing a practical guide to leadership skills. Skills essential in our work and home life. Rarely do leadership books admit mistakes made by the author. Mike's skills developed in the 'school of hard knocks,' which is simply code for learning from our mistakes and our successes. Read the book and you will make fewer mistakes and claim greater success."

— Dave Freudenthal, former governor of Wyoming

"If you didn't have a title, would anyone follow you? The underlying message of this delightful book is that leadership is a choice. In fact, it's hundreds of choices, every day, that revolve around knowing yourself, growing yourself, and then lifting others to do something far more spectacular together than you ever could on your own. Advocating for the kind of leadership our world needs right now, Easley nails it! Apply these principles and become a leader people love to follow."

—Kevin Freiberg, Ph.D.

"Mike is a legend across the Rockies for his leadership, his public service and his humility. He is literally the last person in the region to promote himself. This enduring reputation makes his advice valuable both as food for thought and as a model to emulate."

—Ted Ladd, dean and professor at Hult, instructor at Harvard, and Wyoming entrepreneur

"Mike Easley deftly distills 25 years of CEO experience into a clear, practical, and effective guide for how to avoid the common pitfalls, mistakes, and traps awaiting anyone undertaking a journey into leadership. What's more, readers will emerge enriched and prepared from his counsel on how to become the best version of themselves as a leader—the version worth following!"

—Tim Sullivan, president and CEO, Wright-Hennepin Cooperative Electric Association

"Simply reading this book, I think I became a better person by osmosis! I appreciate Mike's insights, actionable tips on leadership, and writing style. But the real reason I urge you to read this book is because of his humanity, empathy, and heartfelt good intentions. To paraphrase one of my favorite movie lines (Jack Nicholson tells his girlfriend, played by Helen Hunt in the movie *As Good As It Gets,* 'You make me want to be a better man.'): Mike makes me want to be a better leader."

—Susan Fowler, author of *Master Your Motivation*

"Effective leadership requires relentless honesty, focus, and effort. Mike's keen ability to use his own experiences to distill proven leadership techniques paves the way for a new generation of electric co-op leaders."

—Jim Matheson, CEO, National Rural Electric Cooperative Association

BECOMING A LEADER WORTH FOLLOWING

A Practical Guide for Leading Self, Teams, and Organizations

MIKE EASLEY

ISBN 979-8-9900850-0-8 (print)

ISBN 979-8-9900850-1-5 (e-book)

Printed in the United States of America

I dedicate this book to my electric cooperative family.
You all helped me grow out of engineering and grow into leadership.
That growth was painful for me, and maybe for you too.
I'm sure my wake was difficult to navigate in the earlier years,
and I hope it became easier as I grew as a leader.

Becoming A Leader Worth Following *is a noble calling*
and if this book helps you reach that goal, even in some small way,
my journey will have been that much richer and fulfilling.

CONTENTS

PART 1
SELF-MANAGEMENT/SELF-FOCUS   15

CHAPTER 2
Motivation 19

CHAPTER 3
Guiding Forces 33

CHAPTER 4
Self-Awareness

CHAPTER 5
Evaluator/Judgment

PART 2
INTERPERSONAL ABILITY/
TEAM FOCUS 65

CHAPTER 10
Leveraging Teams

CHAPTER 11
Organizational Thinking

CHAPTER 12
The Magic of the Boardroom

PART 4
TOOLS TO SUPPORT
YOUR LEADERSHIP JOURNEY   183

CHAPTER 13
Active Listening and
Motivational Interviewing

CHAPTER 14
The No-Os of Leadership 203

CHAPTER 15
Self-Care for Leaders 219

ACKNOWLEDGMENTS

I would not be where I am today were it not for Ken Blanchard and the Ken Blanchard Executive MBA program at Grand Canyon University. Spending a year in dialogue with Ken Blanchard and his team exploring the essence of leadership is something I will never forget, and is something that has helped and driven me to aspire to become A Leader Worth Following.

In addition, without the support of my friend Kevin Freiberg, I wouldn't have had the courage and guts to take on such a huge challenge nor, at the sunset of my career as an electric cooperative CEO, to put pen to paper to share the story in hopes that others may also embark on their journey in becoming A Leader Worth Following.

FOREWORD

Leaders are learners who teach. What you hold in your hands are the practical, yet hard-won insights from a seasoned executive who would like nothing more than to cut your cycle time on becoming a leader people love to follow and on moving yourself, your team, and your organization to the next level of good.

Mike Easley doesn't write from a position of having arrived. In fact, he would tell you that he is still very much in process—a leadership journey for which there is no destination.

That said, the lessons you are about to learn come from one who has been in the trenches of leadership for over two decades. As the saying goes, "No pressure, no diamond." Mike has felt the pressure of leading a board of directors in a time of crisis, rallying a team facing seemingly insurmountable challenges, changing a tired culture, and figuring out how to serve a community facing significant environmental, technological, political, and social disruption.

Easley has done this in one of the noblest movements in our country: the cooperative movement. Cooperatives are unique in that they were built by the people, for the people. Many are volunteers elected to positions by peers in their communities. From stay-at-home parents to seasoned executives, they bring a wide array of experience or inexperience to the game. These people don't see their organizations as grocery chains, banks, and utilities; they see them as member-centric movements fighting for the "little" person. It takes a special kind of leadership to play and succeed in this arena. Mike Easley has done both.

Frankly, the insights contained here are not new. Unlike so many leadership books that try to be cute by dressing up the same mannequin with different clothes (by which I mean adjectives), Mike takes a straightforward approach to opening the closet door and letting you in on his leadership journey. The takeaways in this book have been tested and they work. I respect that.

Name your arena: business, politics, community, or marriage and family—almost every failure in leadership can be traced back to a failure of nerve. This book calls out that problem and invites you to be courageous.

WARNING! While the ideas here may not be new, putting them into practice is not for the faint of heart. Execution is hard. Easley invites you to discover your blind spots and become self-aware. Of course, this means you have to be vulnerable, courageous, and smart enough to ask for help. The higher you go in an organization, the harder this is because people are less willing to give you feedback. This is why leaders engage trusted advisors like Mike Easley. It's lonely at the top and executives need someone they can talk to, someone they can trust, and someone who will talk straight.

Many years ago, my wife and business partner Jackie and I met Jimmy Blanchard, former CEO of one of the largest credit card processing companies in the world, Synovus Financial. Jimmy was famous for holding all-employee meetings and asking, "What are the 10 dumbest things we do around here, starting with me?" Jimmy was one of those rare CEOs who wanted to become more self-aware and learn how people perceived him.

As Easley so aptly states, "You can't fix a problem if you don't know it exists." Jimmy Blanchard was willing to face the brutal facts of reality, identify the fault lines in his organization, and dig deep to make the necessary changes.

Thanks to the internet, we live in a world of transparency where incidents and behaviors go viral in a heartbeat. It's also a world where people are easily offended. This causes many leaders to armor up, pose, and pretend to be someone they're not for fear that someone—customer/client, board member, regulator, reporter, or employee, just to name a few—will call them out. The problem is that people see right through the façade, and then the leader loses credibility and becomes someone people don't want to follow.

This book calls us all to a higher level of leadership—a leadership that challenges us to give presence to our teammates, to never walk past a problem, to choose service over self-interest, to admit when we are wrong, and then to engage in the art of the apology and find the courage to change. We are invited to trade ego, power, and money for fighting for a cause that enriches lives and makes the world, at least our little corner of it, better.

But in *Becoming A Leader Worth Following*, Mike Easley doesn't leave us there. He gives us the strategies and tools to do it based on what's worked and what hasn't in his own experience as a CEO . . . as a human being.

As a thought leader and practitioner who cares deeply about enriching the lives of others, he is committed to a never-ending search for finding better, more efficient ways to inspire people to change.

—Kevin Freiberg, Ph.D. Co-author of the bestselling books:
*NUTS! Southwest Airlines' Crazy Recipe for Business
and Personal Success; CAUSE! A Business Strategy for
Standing Out in a Sea of Sameness; and Bochy Ball!
The Chemistry of Winning and Losing in
Baseball, Business and Life.*

PREFACE

One of the most important elements of leadership is knowing your story as a leader, what shaped you, where you come from, and then communicating that to your team. It's also important to make a practice of reviewing and keeping in touch with your story. One of the best ways I've found to do this is to create a Leadership Point of View.

I wish I could say that I invented the Leadership Point of View, but I first learned about this approach from Ken Blanchard when I was studying under him for my Ken Blanchard MBA at Grand Canyon University. Through this process, you explore the leadership influences over your life and really home in on your values, your expectations of self and others, and who you are as a leader.

I delivered my Leadership Point of View to my team and incorporated this process into our leadership development program at Powder River Energy during my tenure as CEO, so all our aspiring leaders could create their own Leadership Point of View document. I'm presenting my Leadership Point of View as the preface to this book to honor that practice and to give you an example of what a Leadership Point of View looks like in hopes that you will start yours. The Leadership Point of View is the first step in becoming A Leader Worth Following. After 20 years, I still hope to be that kind of leader and I hope, in some small way, that you, too, may aspire to this journey as you write your own leadership story.

I also hope sharing my Leadership Point of View will help you start to think about how developing your own Leadership Point of View could enhance your leadership abilities and your relationships with your team. More importantly, I wanted to share it to plant the seed that if you find yourself in a position to mentor and lead, or to be part of developing a team or an individual's leadership skills, that you may consider passing on the torch that I picked up from Ken Blanchard and help others aspire towards becoming A Leader Worth Following.

MY LEADERSHIP POINT OF VIEW

My Mentors...

I have been blessed with many mentors in my life, each of them appearing at the right time and place.

When I think about the most influential people in my life, the first person that comes to mind is my maternal grandfather. My grandpa's greatest gift to me was teaching me about work ethic. To my grandpa, the measure of a man was how hard he worked. In my grandpa's opinion, it did not matter if you wore gloves to work or wore a tie. What mattered was that you gave it your all, for as long as it took to get the job done.

He encouraged me to go to college by telling me that he never had the opportunity to attend school past an eighth-grade education. At the same time, he would tell me that 50 cents and my college diploma would get me a cup of coffee. My most memorable experience of my grandpa's leadership style happened on my 13th birthday. My grandpa came into my room at 7:00 a.m., woke me up, and quickly put me to work in the yard filling in ditches. I was crushed that I had to work on my birthday. My grandpa told me that I was a man now and would be working on my birthday for the rest of my life.

Finally, when the day was done at about 4:00 p.m., my grandpa gave me $10. I was totally shocked since my wage working with him during the summer was $1 per day. He must have seen the look on my face because he looked me straight in the eye and said, "Work like a man, get paid like a man." My grandpa was never one for many words.

Jack Hwang was the Grand Master of a tae kwon do school. Mr. Hwang was a very humble and quiet man. I learned the tae kwon do "Aims to Achieve" during the years I was an active student, and internalized them during the years that I taught tae kwon do. Integrity, perseverance, indomitable spirit, courtesy, and self-control are the "Aims to Achieve," or tenets, of tae kwon do. It wasn't until I tested for my fourth-degree black belt that I finally understood that Mr. Hwang's style of leadership required that, in order to achieve mastery, you must humble yourself and serve your students.

The literal translation for tae kwon do is "Hand and Foot Way," but the true meaning of "Way" is the true pearl of wisdom that was passed to me by Mr. Hwang. Most people would assume the meaning of "Way" was direction, manner, or method. While this is partially correct, the true meaning of "Way" is what happens when a doctor helps a patient, a counselor helps a client, a teacher teaches a student, or a parent helps a child with a bruised knee. "Way" is about the basic "helping and healing" of people. In that context, tae kwon do isn't about learning how to use your hands and feet in self-defense, but it's about using your hands and feet in helping, healing, and teaching.

In my professional experience, I have been blessed with wonderful mentors and many of them actually knew that they were mentors to me. Clearly, the most influential person in this area was Doug Bursey. Doug was a huge man both in stature and presence. Most people I knew absolutely hated working for him. Doug had an odd and unnerving way of staring at a person. His gaze would penetrate your soul and any uncertainty you had would reverberate with fear under his scrutiny.

Doug had a way of asking more of you than you thought you were capable of doing. He would throw you in the deep end, and wouldn't come in after you until he sensed you were going down for the third time. When I worked for Doug, I did the impossible and I stretched beyond anything I thought I could do. I was one of the few privileged people that

Doug let see past his crusty, rugged exterior. I saw this side of Doug one evening when we met the bereaved wife of a lineman who had just been fatally injured in an electrical contact accident on the job. From Doug I learned that you could be tough on the outside and tender on the inside.

The strongest mentor in my life has been my maternal grandmother, or Grandma. She is a powerful prayer warrior and has held me accountable to myself and to God. She told me on her 80th birthday that she is finally beginning to see things as they are, and that she was so foolish in her 60s.

My Purpose . . .

At the core of my being is the need to fix things.

The bigger the mess, the more I like it! I also like to solve problems by simply looking at them from a different perspective. Oftentimes, if you are able to convey this perspective to others, you experience that "Aha!" moment. This has occurred numerous times in my business career where I challenged the assumed constraints and did things that couldn't be done according to conventional wisdom. The saying that you should call an expert if you want to find out how not to do something rings true with me. I want to quietly go about making things better. I'm inspired to make a positive difference and to leave things better than how I found them.

My Values . . .

Integrity, Perseverance, Courtesy, Self-Control, and Indomitable Spirit are my core values.

I know I'm living these values when I look at myself in the mirror and feel no twinge of regret or wave of remorse in what I have said, done, or thought.

My father's greatest gift to me was his living example of "taking personal responsibility." My father had struggled since his return from the Vietnam War and didn't find himself until he graduated from college when I was in the ninth grade. Through all the moves from one job to another while I was growing up, my dad never let his family know of his inner demons. Personal responsibility lies at the foundation of my core values, for without this foundation there would be no drive to maintain these values.

Knowing what to avoid as a leader is just as important as knowing how to behave if you aspire to be A Leader Worth Following. I'm firmly convinced that there are three "No-Os" of leadership that create fatal flaws in leadership. These are ego, dinero, and libido. If you can be aware of these No-Os and take personal responsibility for how you lead, you can avoid the carnage of leadership failures involving any one, or a combination of, the No-Os.

My Leadership Vision . . .

I truly want to be A Leader Worth Following.

I have sought leadership positions since I was very young. At first, I liked leadership because of the freedom and the choices due to the sense of being in charge that came with it. Through my young adulthood, I felt as though I deserved to be the leader since I felt competency and commitment to the task at hand were the prerequisites for leadership.

Now in midlife, and definitely past mid-career, I see leadership as a heavy load that, under the right conditions, can be borne easily, but under the wrong circumstances is a crushing burden. I've seen the effect of my decisions played out in the reality of people's lives, and because of that I'm increasingly motivated and inspired to be the best leader I can be—not so much for me, but for the people whose lives I affect as I lead.

My Promise . . .

If people will let me lead them, they can expect that I'll give 110% and I won't quit on them.

I'll hold true to my core values and my faith in both my professional and personal life. I'll try to learn something new every day. I won't ask them to do anything that I wouldn't be willing to do myself. I'll open myself to their feedback and be willing to hear all comments. I won't take their harsh criticism personally; however, I won't be immune to the pain of hurt feelings.

I'll be compassionate as I point out areas for improvement in others and be grateful for having things pointed out to me that I could improve. I'll do my best to help them meet challenges.

My Expectations . . .

I expect my people to be hard-working, honest, and value-centered.

I realize that some people can work harder than others and, on any given day, one's ability to work hard varies. My expectations for them to be honest and value-centered don't vary from person to person, or from situation to situation. I expect people to be honest with themselves as well as with the people around them. I expect people to have compassion for each other and, while it's not so much an expectation, I would very much appreciate them having compassion for me.

My Example . . .

Next to me giving my word, giving my example is the most powerful way I can show my commitment to becoming A Leader Worth Following.

I demonstrate my desire to learn and to grow by looking for ways to learn new things and to revitalize things that I may have overlooked or underused. I keep myself mentally sharp and physically strong by taking care of myself and making positive choices in what I do to and with my body. I learn from my mistakes by admitting them and making a sincere effort to do better next time. I strive to demonstrate integrity in my relationships, my actions, and my decisions.

I invite you to join me as we explore lessons in leadership that have been learned over my life's experience and by attending the "school of hard knocks." We can make the world a better place by doing our part to make ourselves better leaders. If you have just one takeaway from this book, you can make a difference as you journey towards becoming A Leader Worth Following.

I consider myself to be a student of leadership. Although I spent over 20 years as the CEO at PRECorp, I knew, and still know, there are always new things for me to learn as a leader. During my time in the Ken Blanchard MBA program at Grand Canyon University, Ken Blanchard taught me that there is a continuum of leadership, which begins with self-leadership and progresses through team leadership and then to organizational leadership.

This book is designed to support you as you move along that journey. Whether you are aspiring to become a leader, or are in a leadership position and just want to improve your leadership skills, I hope you'll find useful insights and information in the following pages.

Please take a look at the graphic at www.aleaderworthfollowing.com/leaderdevelopment that illustrates the relationship between the focus areas of your leadership journey and the type of skills needed for each. It also shows a continuum of how skills transition and build upon each other as one's leadership focus evolves.

The one constant that takes us through every stage of our leadership journey is the aspiration to become A Leader Worth Following. This is a journey that will never end because, as you'll learn in Chapter 1, Leaders Worth Following are willing to learn, and we can never know everything. I'm still learning as a leader, even after spending more than 20 years as a CEO.

When I first wrote this book, I called it *The No-Os of Leadership*, and I focused on a tool I developed that I and many others have found useful over the years for developing self-awareness as a leader. These No-Os are what I describe as leadership landmines that can take you down as a leader. They are ego, dinero, and libido. The antidotes to these No-Os are self-awareness and empathy. The No-Os have a place on our journeys to becoming Leaders Worth Following, but they are a tool. Chapter 14 of this book is dedicated to the No-Os and how to use them in your own development as a leader. This is also where I share other tools—motivational interviewing, active listening, and self-care—that are essential parts of A Leader Worth Following's skill set.

What prompted me to rewrite this book and reframe it as *Becoming A Leader Worth Following* were two things—the first was what I learned from training and working in mental health counseling. I can't tell you how many times I ran into things during my training that made me say, "I wish I'd have known that when I started leading." I'm still having those moments—this journey is never complete. The second were the comments and feedback I received from readers of *The No-Os of Leadership,* many of whom wanted to take a deeper dive into some of the topics I touched on around becoming A Leader Worth Following, but didn't elaborate on in the first edition.

On a personal level, I wanted to get this book right. I want to start a movement around becoming A Leader Worth Following, and I'd like to invite you to be part of that movement and part of a community of those aspiring to become Leaders Worth Following. My hope is that this book helps us build that community, but in truth if I help just one person with what I've written here, I'll feel as though this book has been a success.

To that end, I'll begin in Chapter 1 by explaining the eight elements that I believe are present when someone is wholeheartedly embracing their journey in becoming A Leader Worth Following. The remainder of this book is separated into four parts, the first three of which discuss the different stages on the leadership continuum.

In Part 1, we begin by exploring the idea of self-leadership. The qualities I highlight here are the necessary foundations for developing as A Leader Worth Following. The concept of self-awareness starts here, but it's a common thread that weaves throughout a leadership journey and one that is present at every point on the leadership continuum.

In Part 2, we discover how to move into effectively leading teams. If you've mastered self-leadership, this step will feel natural. This section of the book covers building and developing teams, and individuals within your teams, while also developing your own experience and abilities as a leader.

In Part 3, we look at organizational leadership and how your approach to leadership needs to change as you shift to this final stage of the continuum where you're leading multiple teams rather than a single team. I also look at the magic that happens in the boardroom and the importance of the board–CEO relationship, particularly in electric cooperatives where I've spent the majority of my professional leadership career.

Finally, in Part 4, I will share some of the tools I believe are most helpful to those of us on our journeys in becoming A Leader Worth Following. The first of these tools are motivational interviewing and active listening, which can significantly improve communication skills, and therefore our relationships with others. This is also where I'll explore the No-Os of Leadership, which are those three areas of ego, dinero, and libido that I believe leaders need to be particularly aware of and avoid if they are to make decisions that truly serve their organization, the people around them, and the greater good. I'll also share what I believe are the six dimensions of self-care, and discuss why it's so important for us as leaders to take care of ourselves.

Throughout this book, I share my own leadership stories and the knowledge I learned from other experiences in my career. I hope that these help put some of the concepts I talk about into context and give you a clearer understanding of how they can manifest along your own leadership journey.

One overarching theme is that becoming A Leader Worth Following is about finding ways to serve your people. These people include not only your employees, but also your customers and external stakeholders. The benefit of having this focus at an organizational level is significant. It leads to greater business success; it leads to a company culture with engaged and thriving employees; and it allows you to develop new leadership talent ready for the challenges every business faces in an increasingly uncertain world.

The concept of service is especially imperative in electric cooperatives, where I spent the majority of my career. These are not-for-profit electric utilities that span the majority of the geographical footprint of the U.S. and have been in existence since 1935. When they were first established, they were a huge part of providing a higher quality of life to people across the rural U.S. Because cooperatives are not-for-profit, they focus on service to their members (customers) as opposed to being served by them.

In order to have a genuine focus on service, the leaders of these organizations and their employees must be thinking about serving, rather than being served. This means the levers that we pull as leaders in a not-for-profit entity focused on service will be much different than the levers leaders pull in a for-profit company focused primarily on the bottom line. My hope is that some of the aspects of my leadership journey presented in this book will help you discover the reasons why you want to lead, how you can be a better leader to your people, and ultimately how you can serve your own members in the best way possible.

> *"Think about your own life and be honest with yourself. Don't you ultimately get your greatest joy, find your deepest meaning, and feel the most 'on purpose' when you are serving— serving your spouse, your kids, your organization, and your community?"*

These days, people are looking for jobs that have meaning, rather than just jobs that make them a living. The approach to leadership and the leadership model that I'll share with you in the following chapters supports the creation of meaning within an organization, and that in turn provides meaning to every individual working within that organization.

Having meaning at work, and the need for Leaders Worth Following, was thrown into sharp relief during the Covid-19 pandemic. The pace of change and the need for great leadership was accelerated during this time. As the world opened up and life returned to some semblance of normal, people and organizations were playing a game of 52-Card Pickup. This game is played by taking a nicely ordered deck of cards and throwing them up in the air. The Covid-19 pandemic took our neatly stacked deck of priorities and tossed them in the air. As people and organizations began picking up those cards, we tossed out ones we didn't need and reordered those we did. The best leaders are cognizant of this and do it with intention and compassion for themselves, their teams, and their organization.

As you move along your leadership journey, I want you to know that you're not alone in facing challenges and issues. Know that there are always solutions to problems you may be facing, even if you're not able to see them just yet. In taking the time and effort to develop yourself as a leader, you're moving one step closer to finding them. Facing issues and challenges is scary, but if you can reframe your thinking to see them as learning opportunities, you'll take a big step forward in your growth journey. Every step you take on this path will bring you closer to your goal of becoming A Leader Worth Following. Although the reality is there is no end goal to achieve or final destination to reach, because on our journeys to become A Leader Worth Following, there will always be more paths to follow around the next corner.

CHAPTER 1

BECOMING A LEADER WORTH FOLLOWING

"The essence of becoming A Leader Worth Following is about leading from a heart of service."

The concept of becoming A Leader Worth Following came to me when I was trying to find the best way of describing what it means to be a servant leader for a keynote address I was giving for the Ken Blanchard Group almost ten years ago. The term *servant leader* has been around for a long time and everyone has their own version of what a servant is. However, not everyone's definition of a servant is the same. While trying to define servant leadership, I realized that this meant people could be talking at cross purposes, even when using the same terms.

When I first learned the term *servant leader* from those at the Ken Blanchard Group, it resonated with me. It's a timeless message, and I believe the idea of being of service to people fits particularly well in today's world. Look back through history, particularly at the likes of religious leaders or figures, and you'll find people who put others first. This archetype of a selfless leader is one we all look for—we all want a selfless leader to follow.

But how do you become that kind of leader? I believe I uncovered the answer while digging deeper into what it means to be a servant leader.

At the heart of being a servant is the word *service*. When you unpack *service*, particularly in the business world, this looks like love for our people, love for our communities, love for our co-workers and love for our customers. And how do we show that love? We do things for them—we perform acts of service. We take care of our families, volunteer in our communities, and help our coworkers and the people on our teams to lead, hopefully, better lives. For me, this is the essence of A Leader Worth Following: one who leads from a heart of service.

The more I thought about what it means to be a servant leader, and in becoming A Leader Worth Following, and the more I reflected on the leaders I've encountered on my leadership journey, the more I realized that Leaders Worth Following all share common traits. I've distilled this into eight elements that are present when someone is truly living their journey in becoming A Leader Worth Following. Each of these under-scores the lessons I've learned in leadership over my career.

Leaders Worth Following . . .

- ▶ Are self-aware

- ▶ Have empathy

- ▶ Are willing to teach

- ▶ Have great expectations and an even greater heart

- ▶ Face reality

- ▶ Own their weaknesses and know how to ask for help

- ▶ Are mentally tough and emotionally predictable

- ▶ Change themselves first

I believe that if, as leaders, we can capture these eight elements and really understand what they are and how to bring them into our lives, then we too are on the path of becoming A Leader Worth Following. A Leader Worth Following is exactly that—someone you want to follow. I know I've had leaders in the past who left the company we worked for and I don't think I'd have followed them wherever they went. I'm sure you've encountered leaders like this too. But I've also had leaders who I want to follow, not because they've imposed their authority on me, but because I trust them. Have you been lucky enough to have one of these leaders on your journey too?

Leaders Worth Following are people you trust, people you feel connected to, and people who will give that little bit of discretionary effort in other parts of our lives. Our experience of being around A Leader Worth Following will, all things considered, be a positive one. It will present an opportunity for us to grow, and we'll feel better for having had the opportunity to be associated with and led by A Leader Worth Following.

As you move through this book, you'll notice that all of these elements weave into the three levels of the leadership continuum that I've identified: self leadership, team leadership and organizational leadership. Before we get started on those, I'll explain each of the eight elements of becoming A Leader Worth Following in a little more detail.

LEADERS WORTH FOLLOWING ARE SELF-AWARE

The first thing that comes to mind when I think of self-awareness is the story of the emperor and his new clothes. I'm sure you're familiar with the tale, whereby a trickster convinces the emperor that he's wearing a really expensive outfit, when the reality is that he's wearing no clothes at all. He has so little self-awareness that he parades through the town naked. The other analogy I frequently use to describe self-awareness is that of the wake you leave behind your leadership "boat."

I discuss leadership wake in much greater detail in both Parts 1 and 2 of this book. In short, A Leader Worth Following is not only aware that they leave a wake, but they are also cognizant of how this affects others and will, therefore, take action to minimize the disruption caused by their wake wherever possible.

Being self-aware doesn't only mean being aware of your impact on those around you; it also means understanding emotions, both your own and those experienced by others. Early on in my career, I used to think of emotions as a bad thing. I believed that you needed to be emotionless when you led—I'm sure it's why Mr. Spock from *Star Trek* was my hero for years. But the challenge with being an emotionless leader is that you miss the ability to tap into things that are unique about the human experience that will help you make better decisions—your emotions and gut feelings.

Many people, not only leaders, are unaware of the eight basic emotions and their relationship with them. However, even if we're unaware of these emotions on a conscious level, we still feel them. These eight basic emotions are actually pairs; each has an opposite. They are:

- ▸ Anger—Fear

- ▸ Disgust—Trust

- ▸ Sadness—Joy

- ▸ Surprise—Anticipation

To illustrate why being aware of our emotions and being able to identify them is so important, let's look at the Anger–Fear pairing as an example. In modern Western culture, men are taught not to show weakness; it's seen as negative. However, the problem is that when you feel fear, you also feel weak and society has told you that, as a man, you shouldn't feel weak. If you don't understand and explore your fear, you'll turn to its opposite: anger.

In reality, feeling fear at times is normal, for both men and women. Just imagine how different our society would be if everybody understood that anger was the opposite of fear, and had the self-awareness to sit with their fear and not be freaked out by it to the point that they resort to anger. Leaders who are self-aware and understand these eight basic emotions don't become angry when they face uncertainty because they are able to understand that they're feeling fear and can examine their emotions without becoming overwhelmed by them. This not only enables them to make better decisions, but also means they are more emotionally predictable when working with their teams.

LEADERS WORTH FOLLOWING HAVE EMPATHY

If you don't have empathy then it means you don't really care about the people you're working with, the wake that you're leaving, or helping others develop and grow to become the best person they can be. To work on becoming more self-aware, you need to care about both yourself and others, which is why self-awareness and empathy support one another.

I'll explain the concept of empathy in greater detail in Chapter 6, and explore the difference between empathy and sympathy. For now, all you need to understand is that empathy means joining someone where they are. The concept of mirror neurons is also important when it comes to empathy. Recent neuroscience research (for example, Bonini et al.'s 2022 study "Mirror Neurons 30 Years Later: Implications and Applications" in the journal, *Trends of Cognitive Sciences*; https://doi.org/10.1016/j.tics.2022.06.003) has found that when we are communicating with another person and are in tune with them emotionally, we feel what they feel. When this happens, the same part of our brain lights up as theirs, effectively "mirroring" what they are feeling.

The reason it's important to understand mirror neurons is that, when you are self-aware, you are able to recognize that this is what's happening and that the emotions you're feeling may not be yours. When you know these are emotions that someone else is projecting onto you, it allows you to put yourself in their place without actually *being* in their place, and this takes a lot of the power out of the emotions you feel as a result. When those are emotions like stress, anxiety, or anger, it's particularly important that you are able to distance yourself from them so that you remain calm and behave appropriately.

LEADERS WORTH FOLLOWING ARE WILLING TO TEACH

As much as Leaders Worth Following are willing to teach, they are also willing to learn. The reason I mention learning is because if we don't want to learn or if we believe we've learned it all, then we aren't going to be much of a teacher. In my experience, the best teachers are people who are curious and always learning themselves. When they learn new things, they want to share them with other people.

As I mentioned in my Leadership Point of View in the Preface, I have trained in tae kwon do and, like all martial arts, you work your way through different colors of belts as you progress, starting at white and moving through the full spectrum of colors until you reach black—which represents all the colors combined. Once you achieve your black belt, you progress in what are called "dans," and the way you earn each new dan is not by learning more yourself but by teaching others. The reason that you teach is that this allows you to learn everything all over again as you truly learn it for the first time.

This isn't only true in the world of martial arts. It's a universal truth that if you want to truly learn any topic, the best way to do so is to teach it. So if you really want to be a great leader, teach leadership—and beyond that, if you want to journey towards becoming A Leader Worth Following, teach others how to do the same.

LEADERS WORTH FOLLOWING HAVE GREAT EXPECTATIONS AND AN EVEN GREATER HEART

These two elements balance one another well. When we have great expectations, this means we have expectations of ourselves and hold ourselves to a high standard. We also inspire others by having great expectations for them. We help others learn, we help them stretch themselves, and we encourage and support them to do things that we know they can do, even if they are unsure of their own abilities.

MIKE'S LEADERSHIP LESSON: I BELIEVE IN YOU

Early on in my career, I took a job as an engineering manager working for Doug Bursey, whom I mentioned in my Leadership Point of View, at a tiny cooperative electrical utility in Alaska. This cooperative provided power for two towns that were 120 miles apart—Glennallen and Valdez. What lay between these two towns was beautiful, but unforgiving, nature. There were mountains, lakes, and forests, and it wasn't easy to travel between them.

Glennallen and Valdez were connected by a powerline and supported one another by exchanging electrical power throughout the year. Valdez had a hydropower plant, which meant they generated power during the summer. In the winter, it was the diesel generators in Glennallen that helped serve the power needs of both communities. In between the two towns was a substation, which could be accessed via a remote-control system; it wasn't easy to make the 60-mile journey to the substation itself.

About one week into the job, Doug called me: "Hey Mike, Pump 12 (that substation I just described) is down and the remote control is down. We need you to fix it."

"Well Doug, I wish I could, but I've only been here a week and I really don't know anything about that system yet . . ." I replied.

"You're an engineer! I've put all the manuals and equipment in my car and I'm on my way to pick you up. You're going to go and fix it." With that, Doug hung up.

All I could think at that moment was, "Holy crap." True to his word, Doug arrived with all the manuals and equipment, picked me up and dropped me off 60 miles into the Alaskan wilderness at the substation. I worked all night, reading the manuals and trying different things. Eventually, the substation started working again—in all honesty I've always thought it just started up on its own, and to this day I don't know what I did to get it working again.

Doug was impressed though, and I never told him that I didn't know exactly what I'd done!

Leadership Lessons . . .

This is a great example of a leader who expected the seemingly impossible from one of his people. Doug expected that I would be able to fix the substation. I told him that I didn't know how, and he supported me by providing me with the manuals and tools I'd need, as well as showing that he believed in my abilities. He stretched me outside of my comfort zone and I succeeded—had he not had those great expectations of me, I wouldn't even have attempted to fix the substation.

You can support your people in a similar way—tell them that it's okay if they don't succeed or have all the answers. Use phrases like, "This might be impossible, but I think you can do it," or, "You've never done this before, so let's see how close you can get." Or if someone comes to you and tells you they don't know the answer, you can respond with, "There is no absolute right answer, that's not what we're solving for. What I'm looking for is your best answer."

Leaders who have great expectations of their people pull the best out of them, but these expectations have to be tempered by having empathy and being self-aware. You have to know when your people are drowning (overwhelmed) and you need to reach in and pull them out. This is what having a greater heart is all about. You have to show people your kindness and tenderness; you have to help them see your personal humanity. When you do, they won't be scared when you ask them to do the impossible because they'll know that you're capable of understanding them and feeling their pain. They can see and feel that you have a big heart.

> Great expectations and an even greater heart need to go together in order to bring the best out of people in a constructive way that builds confidence. When you show someone you believe in them, but acknowledge their challenges, you'll be amazed at what they can achieve.

This element of being A Leader Worth Following involves being vulnerable. To be a truly authentic leader, vulnerability isn't something you can turn on and off, you have to first know that you have a soft spot (which is where self-awareness and empathy feeds in) and then you have to let your people see your soft spot.

LEADERS WORTH FOLLOWING FACE REALITY

The first reality all Leaders Worth Following have to face is about themselves—you aren't omnipotent. As a leader, you aren't perfect. You're human just like everybody else; you don't know all the answers, you'll make mistakes and that's OK. When talking about servant leadership, Ken Blanchard says, "Servant leaders don't think less of themselves, they just think of themselves less." This speaks to putting aside your ego and being able to face the reality that you don't come first.

Another crucial aspect of facing reality is being able to accept feedback, even when that feedback is really difficult to hear. You have to receive feedback with an open mind and a degree of curiosity. As I mentioned when talking about Leaders Worth Following being willing to teach, this curiosity has to begin with yourself. Question why you do certain things, and dig into what's truly going on in any given situation. All the elements of A Leader Worth Following that I have already laid out work together to help you face reality.

What's more, by modeling your ability to be open to feedback, even when that feedback is uncomfortable, you'll encourage the people around you to embrace feedback in a similar way.

LEADERS WORTH FOLLOWING OWN THEIR WEAKNESSES AND KNOW HOW TO ASK FOR HELP

This is an essential step that comes once you face your reality, because when you're honest with yourself, your reality might tell you that things aren't very good at the moment. Owning our weaknesses means we accept responsibility for our own issues and don't put them onto other people, especially those we are leading. The next step is to address our weaknesses: to do something about them. This is where asking for help comes in.

Leaders who aren't afraid of their weaknesses and who know how to ask for help inspire people. When you are open about your weaknesses and ask for help, people will want to be led by you because they see that you're continually improving and, therefore, realize that you'll help them do the same. To be vulnerable in this way, we need that self-aware-ness and empathy to ensure that when we show others our weaknesses, it doesn't make us feel weak and feed into a sense of fear or anger. We need to know ourselves deeply and understand our emotions so that we can regulate them and use them to help ourselves and our teams.

LEADERS WORTH FOLLOWING ARE MENTALLY TOUGH AND EMOTIONALLY PREDICTABLE

Following from being able to own our weaknesses and asking for help is the seventh element of being A Leader Worth Following—being mentally tough and emotionally predictable. All leaders need a healthy dose of resiliency, especially in today's world. For me, being mentally tough means being able to withstand being uncomfortable for a while.

Often it feels as though society doesn't want us to feel uncomfortable and makes being uncomfortable a bad thing, when the reality is that being uncomfortable is part of life, and when we can push through that discomfort, it often leads to better things. Think of a yoga practice as an example—the poses you hold feel uncomfortable, but when you hold them through that discomfort, you find a release that simply isn't possible without dealing with that discomfort first.

It's important, however, that we don't confuse the concept of toughness with being unbending or unyielding. Toughness is about having flexibility so that we are able to withstand external forces acting on us without breaking. As leaders, being mentally tough and able to function when we are uncomfortable is important, but so too is being emotionally predictable for our people.

Emotional predictability doesn't mean that we can't have moments where we let off steam, but it does mean that we make sure we let off steam at an appropriate time. Uncertainty is something that most of us find challenging to deal with, so when we are emotionally predictable as leaders, we remove a layer of uncertainty in any situation. The people around us will, therefore, know how we will react and how we are going to behave, which in turn gives everyone room and safety to function well. I'll talk more about how you can cultivate emotional control and therefore deliver that emotional predictability in Chapter 4.

LEADERS WORTH FOLLOWING CHANGE THEMSELVES FIRST

All of the elements I've discussed here are things we should be working on in ourselves first. None of them are a destination; they are all part of a journey—our leadership journey. One thing I've observed on my own leadership journey and in my interactions with other leaders is that it's incredibly difficult, if not impossible, to ask other people to change if you're not willing to change yourself.

If you want to teach your people the path of becoming A Leader Worth Following, the best way to do so is by modeling that behavior and embracing it. All eight elements of becoming A Leader Worth Following come from within you—and when you are able to put in the work in each of those areas, you'll notice that those around you often start doing the same. It's fitting, then, that we begin our exploration of what it takes to become A Leader Worth Following by diving into your leadership foundation: self-management, focus, and leadership.

PART 1

SELF-MANAGEMENT/ SELF-FOCUS

As I've said, your journey as a leader starts by leading yourself. The concepts of self-management and self-focus are important to create the awareness needed for being a leader. Your personal growth journey may not be one that is focused on being formally recognized as a leader, but everyone can benefit from growth opportunities around self-leadership.

Even as a young child, there are opportunities for leadership. Maybe you were the kid who organized games, or maybe you were the kid who laid out the rules. Even in play, these are real steps along the journey of leadership.

As you get older, things begin to get a little more formal. You'll have different opportunities, whether through school or extracurricular activities. When you look at the people who naturally take to being leaders early on, you can identify some common characteristics among them. These people usually have lots of focus, they're able to self-regulate, they have self-discipline, and they know what they want. True leaders genuinely care about other people and truly want to help them.

Although you could argue that most people know what they want, the people who develop most quickly as leaders not only know what they want, but they also have the focus and desire to go after it and do what they need to do to work toward it. This is where the qualities of self-management and self-focus come into play.

When we go into the workplace, most of us don't start at the top. We have to work our way up through the ranks, learning our job or profession as we go. However, the qualities of self-management and self-focus help you to stand out and be recognized by the leaders in any organization, and your ability to work well with others and support and serve your team lays the foundation for your leadership journey.

Good leaders are constantly looking at their people to find those who have the most potential, and then coaching them along their leadership journey. In doing so, they are helping the Leader-Worth-Following movement.

Focusing on yourself and understanding your motivation helps get you recognized, and your desire to serve others will set you apart. This creates a virtuous cycle where the characteristics of focus, self-discipline, dependability, and service ensure you're recognized. You are then fed work and opportunities to continue your development of those skills and become better at what you do.

> *"The greatest character strength and the greatest virtue is Love. And what does love look like? It looks like* Service.*"*

I believe all leaders need to be highly self-aware. The first step on any leadership journey starts with managing yourself and displaying those qualities of focus, self-discipline, dependability, and, most importantly, service.

If you're a first-time leader, or an aspiring leader, the first thing to do to move along your leadership journey and to start having increased responsibilities is to show that you're effective at leading yourself. Being aware of this need to have optimal motivation, being self-disciplined and dependable, and working on developing these qualities, is important if you want to aspire to greater leadership positions on your journey to become A Leader Worth Following.

If you already hold a leadership position, it's good to reflect on where you've been on your journey. Even if you're only leading a few people, it's important to reflect on how you got to where you are, especially if you want to continue to grow as a leader and take on higher levels of responsibility and service to your teams.

In my opinion, one of a leader's jobs is to develop their team and give their people opportunities for continued growth. If you have folks on your team who you feel have leadership potential, helping them understand how their self-leadership will prepare them for their own journey is an important part of your role. This compliments your own development toward becoming A Leader Worth Following. If you're aspiring to greater levels of responsibility and leadership, your ability to tell stories and describe some of the things that have helped you develop as a leader is also important.

We'll begin exploring these qualities in Chapter 2 by discussing what I believe are four of the most important characteristics to develop for self-management and self-awareness: motivation, self-discipline, dependability, and service to others.

>>>>>>>>>>>>>>>>>>>>>>>>>>>>>>>>>>>>>

CHAPTER 2

MOTIVATION

"The positive effects of optimal motivation will give you energy and the ability to keep going when others might give up."

Motivation is why people do what they do. We all have motivation. Understanding what your motivators are can help you get things done and accomplish the goals you've set for yourself.

When we're thinking about motivators in terms of ourselves, it quickly becomes clear that understanding our motivators helps us to accomplish our goals and even has an effect on our internal conversations. Susan Fowler, author of *Master Your Motivation*,[1] discusses the new science of optimal motivation and identifies three things that produce it: choice, connection, and competence. Creating choice, connection, and competence will serve you well in your leadership journey. When it comes to starting your leadership journey, there are three elements that will help you stay on track: focus, self-regulation, and dependability.

Focusing on what you want in spite of distractions is necessary in order to accomplish anything. Self-regulation is about remembering what it is you want to achieve and being able to intentionally avoid the things

---

[1]Susan Fowler, *Master Your Motivation: Three Scientific Truths* (Oakland: Berrett-Koehler Publishers, 2019).

that take you off track in the pursuit of that goal. Dependability is about being consistent and knowing that you can rely on yourself and that others can rely on you.

Others also need to see these three qualities in you. They need to know they can rely on you to stay on course through your self-regulation and that you have enough focus to keep your eye on the target to avoid getting distracted along the way. Leaders should understand and develop these three elements within themselves right from the beginning of their leadership journey.

BUILDING BLOCKS FOR LEADERSHIP

Focus, self-regulation, dependability, and service are characteristics that people will recognize in you quite early on in your leadership journey. Anyone who has these qualities—whether in the workplace or elsewhere, whether young or old—will be easy to lead. This is what will get you noticed as a potential future leader.

If you're leading a team, and notice a person who has more focus, more self-regulation, and more dependability than another, you'll rely on them to help get things done. This, in turn, sets the stage for them to become a leader, whether formally or informally, in the future.

The concepts of focus, self-regulation, dependability, and service don't really change, regardless of what stage you're at in your leadership journey. What may change, however, are the things underneath those characteristics. What creates that focus might be different in your 20s than in your 40s, for instance.

Dependability might look different early in your career than it does later on. Early on, it may be as simple as showing up when you've committed to do so. As you grow in your work and position, the idea of dependability is still there, but it might look different compared to those early stages of your career. Later on, dependability might include being able to complete your work by delegating items to your team.

While the way these qualities are displayed might change, what doesn't change is the necessity of having these qualities in the first place. If you don't have focus, self-regulation, dependability, and service, you won't really be able to get out of the blocks to begin your journey towards becoming A Leader Worth Following. Let's unpack each of these qualities a little further.

FOCUS

Focus varies from person to person, but the way I describe it is as a sense of positive urgency that builds inside a person to help them move towards an end goal. This sense of positive urgency can be fed in different ways, depending on what's going on in your life. If your sense of urgency is fear-based, your motivation will be suboptimal. If your urgency comes from a need to please, you might be struggling with forming healthy connections. Perhaps your urgency is based on a lack of confidence, in which case you might have some challenges related to competency. The best motivation comes from positive urgency that links to your purpose and values, contributes to the welfare of others, and involves learning and growth for yourself and others. As humans we tend to function along a continuum where we are in motion towards a goal, aspiration, or outcome. Perhaps your motivation is not optimal all the time, but you do the work to be self-aware and feed yourself healthy self-talk to develop a mindset that brings with it choices, connection, and competence.

For example, you or a team member may have a really high desire to please others and be recognized for a job well done. While feeling motivated to get things done, this type of suboptimal motivation may lead to feeling depleted. Instead consider shifting your thinking about the job by recognizing choices, how it helps people, and how you may grow from it. This type of motivation, optimal motivation, will give you energy and fill you up.

We all have responsibilities in our personal lives that we're trying to fulfill, whether that's providing for our families or providing for ourselves. That can help us stay focused as well. For other people, their focus can come from a belief about how the world needs to look or behave in relation to a particular issue.

It's not only having this focus that tends to make people good leaders, but also being aware of that focus and what's behind it. One person may be inspired by multiple factors in their lives, and it won't always be the same thing that they focus on every day. Someone who is aware of the importance of creating choice, connection and competency in themselves and others will create optimal motivation for themselves and others. The positive effects of optimal motivation will give you energy and the ability to keep going when others might give up.

Some days might be more difficult than others and you might need to draw on different aspects of those elements to compel you through the day, the week, or to get to the end of a project. Drawing from an aligned set of values, a noble purpose and the love of serving others will be helpful to get through these days. As you're trying to develop as A Leader Worth Following, it's essential to be aware of what is important to you so that you can tap into these optimal motivators to keep yourself moving, focused, and filled with positive energy.

Being able to identify what is important to others is also helpful when you're leading them, because you'll be looking for the next leaders you can develop. By understanding how other people will help you, as the leader, to do a better job of developing those future leaders and giving them opportunities. It's important to balance what's important to us in addition to the needs of others and how we can all serve the common good.

UNDERSTAND YOURSELF FIRST

Understanding yourself first is the key to being able to motivate and manage yourself. Understanding the power of framing things through the lens of choice, connection, and competence can feed your motivators. You can use this mindset to help you be present and be at your best—an essential step to take before you can lead others and critical if you want others to willingly follow where you lead.

Be mindful as to how your leadership style may affect others as you follow your leadership journey. There are many ways to manage and lead. Without self-awareness, focus may not always be helpful.

For example, imagine you're driving a speedboat racing across the water, and that you're the kind of person who leaves a pretty big wake behind you. As your boat goes by, it creates big waves that rock and crash into everything around them, knocking people over. If you're the kind of person who leaves a big wake behind them that disrupts other people, whether you're in a leadership position or just self-leading, it's a sign that you're not entirely aware of yourself and that your focus may not be healthy for either you or the people around you.

This links back to the concepts of self-awareness and self-focus. If you understand yourself and your motivation and you're aware of your effect on others, it helps you as a leader. This self-awareness also encompasses some of the other characteristics you need to develop for self-leadership that we'll talk about later in this first part. Responsibility, in particular, springs to mind because it's your personal responsibility to make sure you don't leave a damaging wake as you move through life and work.

SELF-REGULATION

In simple terms, focus is remembering why you're doing something and what you're trying to accomplish, as well as how you're going to achieve your goal. Self-regulation is discerning the thoughts and actions that keep you moving forward along your chosen path. Self-awareness can help you remember what you want, analyze what you're doing to get there, and then make the adjustments needed to keep yourself on track.

Your values are one element underpinning your self-regulation. As a leader, and especially an early leader or self-leader, it's important to understand the values and ethics that are guiding you as you move through life. The life lessons you've learned, your behaviors, and ways of thinking about things over time, translate into values.

One value that might guide you is being truthful, for example. I think we all learn at an early age that being truthful helps us accomplish our goals and get what we need in the long run. As we've gone through our lives, most of us have discovered that being truthful is the better path.

If we look at the idea of self-regulation in the context of the value of truth, we remember that being truthful is important. We know that it will help us accomplish our goal, and we've learned that things work out better by being truthful. Therefore, when we're given the opportunity, we choose to be truthful. The self-regulation comes in when we choose this path even when it might be easier to hide, avoid, or shade the truth. Remembering that being truthful is important to us and important for our outcomes is an act of self-awareness.

Of course, there are many other values; truth is just one of them. The point is that, when you have self-regulation, you're able to take the things you've learned on your life's journey—either through experience or observation—and apply those values consistently to your actions and choices.

Self-regulation involves identifying the behaviors that help us accomplish our goals and work well with others, and then applying them. Dependability, which I'll talk more about shortly, is another example that comes to mind.

We have to practice self-regulation in many areas of our lives. We're constantly bombarded by many distractions in our daily lives, and we need to remember to focus on our true goals and not the diversions that may be taking our attention. It could be our phones, Facebook messages, or any other number of interruptions. Being aware of those distractions and not allowing them to draw our focus takes self-regulation.

As a leader, if you look at somebody and can see they have focus, a purpose, and are motivated to accomplish a goal or task—as well as having the self-regulation to remember both why that goal is important and what they need to do to accomplish that goal—you're likely to see them as dependable.

You can count on them to not only have the ability to accomplish goals, but also to keep focused in a positive direction. As soon as they do this consistently, they become dependable. This makes it easy for people to give them greater responsibility.

If having increased responsibility and levels of leadership is important to you, you would do well to understand how focus and self-regulation help you consistently reach or work toward the final goal. Ultimately, this comes across as dependability, because people will see they can count on you to get things done.

DEPENDABILITY

The hallmark of dependability is consistency and being consistent over time. As a leader, people are counting on you and, therefore, you need to be dependable. In the context of self-leadership, dependability is coming to work on time, being available when you need to be, and saying "yes" when you're asked to do something.

Of course, any characteristic, if taken to the extreme, can be overdone. Even though being dependable is an excellent quality, it could conflict with your priorities. For example, if you take on work outside of regular business hours, are you dependable at home? Or do you prioritize work above all else? There has to be a balance.

I believe that leaders need to be aware of how to take care of themselves. If you give everything to your work or your company, there will be aspects of your personal life that don't work out so well. Ultimately this catches up with you and creates issues with your work and your personal life.

As you move along your leadership journey, from leading yourself to leading teams to leading organizations, the demands on you increase as the responsibility increases. You have to make sure you take care of yourself and keep this in balance with other aspects of your life.

While dependability is certainly about saying "yes," it might also be about saying "no."

If you're aspiring to lead, you should understand the qualities people look for as they develop leaders and give them more responsibility. Keep these characteristics in mind when you're making decisions about how you go about your work day, or even how you go about your life. We've discussed focus, self-discipline, and dependability in the context of self-leadership, but having a heart of service will make all the difference as you move beyond self-leadership and take greater steps towards becoming A Leader Worth Following.

SERVICE

Service isn't about taking on the role of a servant and becoming less; it's about taking on the role and being more. Serving yourself might feel good for the short term, but in the long run we find ourselves experiencing the greatest joy and the most satisfaction when we are serving others. As I said in Chapter 1, the concept of becoming A Leader Worth Following came to me from a place of service.

As you develop your skills as a self-leader, you'll be working with other people. You will be living in a community with yourself, your co-workers, your family, your friends, and people you may never know. Opportunities to help others will abound, and it's through serving others that you'll learn much about yourself. Don't get me wrong; I'm not saying that you sacrifice yourself in service to others. In order for you to grow as a leader, it's important to focus on those around you: how you impact them, how they impact you, and how you can work together to make a difference at work, at home, and in the community.

FOCUS ON THESE CHARACTERISTICS TO PROGRESS AS A LEADER

Many businesses strongly focus on skills competence, which often means people who are best at a particular task seem to find their way into leading others to do that task. But once you want to move beyond this level of team leadership, and move along the continuum of leading bigger teams, leading departments, and then leading organizations, it becomes essential to be aware of these characteristics.

If you aren't in a leadership position yet, but you want to move in that direction and are struggling to get there, I would advise you to look not only at the elements we've discussed in this chapter, but also at the ones that come in the following chapters of Part 1.

Take some time to assess where you are in each of those elements. Chances are that if you're not progressing within leadership, and you can't seem to get past leading a small team or feel stuck, you'll find the answers you're looking for within these characteristics. If you pay some attention to the characteristics discussed in Part 1 and work on those areas, you could move past that sticking point because a lack of awareness in these areas is what's been holding you back.

> *"Leaders Worth Following are mentally tough and emotionally predictable. They are a rock for their people and the organization. They need to be tough as nails, but tender of heart."*

THE STARTING POINT FOR YOUR LEADERSHIP JOURNEY

Understanding motivation is really important. As I said earlier in the chapter, the same things may not motivate you every day, and sometimes what inspires you to be effective one day won't be what inspires you to be effective the next. We should be able to quickly shift our thinking in order to keep ourselves optimally motivated. Looking for ways to create choice, connection, and competence will help us maintain the best type of motivation. Learn to shift your perspective and look at a situation through the lens of these optimal motivators.

By understanding your motivators and remembering what's important to you, you can consciously find the right motivation for each day. If you're not feeling particularly motivated, it could be that you're focusing on only one aspect of what motivates you. Having the ability to find or create the right motivation for yourself each day is an essential skill as a leader.

For example, imagine that it's important for you to make a good living for your family. One day, you win the lottery or receive a windfall inheritance. All of a sudden, making a good living for your family isn't as urgent as it was before. If your only motivator is money, you have to consider what's important to you if money is no longer an issue. This is why being aware of creating choice, connection, and building competency is important for optimal motivation.

Having that awareness about various motivators allows you shift your thinking to find your most compelling motivators at any given point in time to inspire you to do your best work.

The four characteristics I've talked about in this chapter—focus, self-regulation, dependability, and service—are just the first characteristics you have to explore as you develop on your journey of becoming A Leader Worth Following. All the characteristics we're going to explore in Part 1 build on each other.

Think of it like a continuum. We've started with focus, self-regulation, dependability, and service. Next, we're going to explore responsibility and independence. In Chapter 4, we'll dive into emotional control and self-esteem. Finally, as we finish Part 1, we'll come to critical thinking. Each one underpins the others and they are all equally important.

MIKE'S LEADERSHIP LESSON: SCOUTING

"Roger, my feet really hurt! I think I'm getting blisters . . ."

"Ahh, geez Jon, let's sit on this rock for a second and see if we can't do something about that! I remember getting blisters on my first hiking trip in the mountains so I know how sore your feet can be after a day of walking the trails," Roger said, rummaging in his pack looking for a Band-Aid.

"Won't we lose the others if we stop?"

"Don't you worry about that, I know where we're going, and once we patch your feet up, I'm sure we'll catch them easily," Roger said with a wink.

I'm sure there were many interactions like this between our two Scout leaders, Roger and Chris, during our 50-mile hike in the Kiamichi Mountains in southeast Oklahoma. About 50 kids ranging in age from 12–17 participated, and we walked about 10 miles per day over five days. There was no defined trail system; all the hiking was back-country, and we navigated with maps and compasses.

When I was younger, I was in Scouting and felt drawn to leadership. At the time, I think my desire for leadership was about directing things towards what I wanted or what I thought was best. It was about me rather than serving others. I had a great time being a patrol leader and in organizing things I wanted to do, but I felt like I was missing something. It was on this 50-mile hike that I learned something special about leadership.

Roger and Chris walked around, mingling with the hikers. They had a sense of each hiker and an idea of how they were doing. Everyone experienced fatigue, blisters, equipment issues, hunger, thirst, homesickness, and plenty more concerns. Roger and Chris knew how to deal with all these issues. They told everyone that they themselves had experienced similar challenges. They explained how they dealt with the various challenges. They connected kids by suggesting they buddy up, and oftentimes the kid who needed a pair of dry socks was a buddy for the day with someone who brought too many socks.

Each morning, either Roger or Chris was missing when we all woke up and had breakfast. They would mysteriously reappear somewhere on the trail, usually around lunch. After we finished lunch, one of them would always hang back to make sure our break area was returned to "normal." Although we were try-ing to "take only pictures and leave only footprints," 50 kids left a mess, even after they thought they had cleaned things up. Whichever one of them who hung back would usually arrive in camp an hour or more after the group stopped for the day. They always seemed to bring a few hikers with them.

About a year after this experience, I had a conversation with Chris about their actions. He explained that one of them would get up super early and essentially set the trail for the group. They were familiar with the route, but things could have changed since the last time they were on the trail. The lone hiker could cover much more ground than the group, and they would hike as far as they could but return in time to meet up for lunch. The person that stayed behind after lunch would invariably pick up stragglers and help them finish the day's hike. This process made sure every Scout made it to the stopping point, and that the slowest Scouts had just as much support as the fastest ones. Keep in mind that this was before the days of cell phones and affordable hand-held radios.

Leadership Lessons . . .

As Scout leaders, Roger and Chris exhibited all the qualities I've talked about in this chapter. They had focus to keep all of us Scouts motivated and moving each day. They showed self-discipline in always being the first to rise and the last to go to bed. They were dependable. We all knew we could count on them to support us on that 50-mile hike.

Being a Scout, of course, taught me to be prepared. Beyond that though, I learned that the best leaders are not always at the front of the pack. You'll sometimes find them at the front, in the middle, and at the back, lending a helping hand and being of service to their co-workers, friends, family, and community.

Self-awareness and empathy got 50 scouts to complete (and mostly enjoy!) a 50-mile, back-country hike. Possessing and demonstrating these traits will help you on your journey to become A Leader Worth Following.

CHAPTER 3

GUIDING FORCES

"Responsibility and independence go hand-in-hand to propel a developing leader towards higher levels of leadership."

In the previous chapter, we talked about characteristics that set people apart and help them get ready for leadership. Guiding forces are also elements that set you apart, but I would describe these as an internal mechanism that helps keep you on the rails as you're starting to lead, rather than external qualities. There is some overlap here with self-discipline, but I believe there are two important guiding forces that will help set you apart and set you up for your leadership journey: responsibility and independence.

RESPONSIBILITY

From a leadership perspective, the idea of responsibility is that you feel called to a higher level of accountability to both yourself and the people around you. This begins early in your leadership journey. It's exhibiting responsibility towards the things that are very close to you, which can include yourself as well as your teammates.

As you progress along your leadership journey by learning more about leading yourself, then leading teams and eventually leading organizations, that sphere of responsibility becomes larger as your job changes.

People who are natural leaders tend to step up and take responsibility when there's a job that needs to be done and everyone else is just standing around. When you're developing as a leader, you're the person who jumps in and takes personal responsibility, not only for doing things but also for the problems that come up.

Challenges or problems arise in both long-term projects and in our day-to-day work. A Leader Worth Following will take responsibility for that problem and work to fix it, rather than complain about it or point fingers. This means they take action when faced with a challenging situation, rather than freezing or simply giving up and saying, "This is somebody else's problem, not mine." They take ownership of the challenge or problem, and it becomes theirs to resolve. Taking personal responsibility is an important quality of leadership.

While we can't change other people, or necessarily fix situations that belong to other people, someone who is a natural leader will assume they can do something. Even if they can't do everything, they will tackle the elements that they can. More often than not, that's enough to keep the project going or moving in the right direction.

Within the context of your leadership journey, responsibility means that you'll feel a personal responsibility to get things done or deal with situations as they arise, and you won't give up when faced with barriers. In fact, it's more than likely that you'll be the person figuring out how to overcome those barriers. Responsibility, in this sense, ties in closely with the second guiding force, independence.

INDEPENDENCE

Deciding to take responsibility for something is one thing, but you also need to have a sense of independence or agency to empower you to think that you can actually *take* responsibility.

For example, this isn't about relying on others to solve the problem or find the answers to questions you may have. Early on in your career, when you're trying to figure things out, you might feel as though you have to return to your supervisor for help. If you're independent, the difference is that you're not going back to your supervisor about every possible question you have with a project. You take initiative to find the answers on your own.

In other words, if you can't do everything, do *something*. You see yourself as empowered enough to take some action, even if there are elements that you still need support with.

However, there may be situations where you may not feel you have the authority to do something. In those cases, approach your supervisor with options to solve the problem. After doing this a few times, your supervisor will most likely give you the room you need to make the necessary decisions. Being able to take action even when you are uncomfortable is a sign of growing independence. Knowing what actions get you closer to the end result is a sign of growing competence. You should be aware of your own competence, and seek guidance when you're unsure about it, while at the same time growing your independence.

COMBINING RESPONSIBILITY WITH INDEPENDENCE

Responsibility and independence go hand-in-hand to propel a developing Leader Worth Following towards higher levels of leadership. If you're part of a team, or just a sole worker, and you're able to demonstrate and use these guiding forces, you'll begin to build your competencies in these areas.

This is true whether you naturally take responsibility and feel that you have the autonomy to make things happen on your own, or whether you understand that these are important qualities to demonstrate and therefore look for opportunities to take responsibility and be independent. In my experience, when you start to do these things, you'll find that people start seeing you as a natural leader and turn to you to help move things along and organize and accomplish tasks.

MIKE'S LEADERSHIP LESSON: MY FIRST JOB AFTER COLLEGE

"Beep-beep-beep!" My hand reached out and hit the button on the alarm clock as I stretched and sat up. I didn't delay getting out of bed or feel tempted to fall back to sleep. I was excited to get up, start my day, and get to work. You see, this was my first "real" job and I had two choices: I could be at home chomping at the bit to go to work, or I could just go in.

I started my professional career straight out of college as a transmission design engineer at an electric cooperative that generated and transmitted electricity and sold that power to distribution cooperatives. When I started, I went to work early and I tended to stay late.

When I say arrived early, I mean around 7:00 a.m. I was in a brand-new position and I was learning my job, so when I arrived in the morning, I'd line up my day. I looked at the projects I had and gave myself time to wrap my head around the tasks that I needed to get done that day, or examined areas where I predicted problems or potential challenges.

By the time my colleagues started their days, I was already working. I always found it interesting that those people looked at me strangely and asked what I was doing at work so early. For me, it felt natural. I was taking responsibility for my work and ensuring that I knew what needed to be done and could do it.

When you're brand new in a position, you may not know everything that you need to know; I certainly didn't at that stage, and you shouldn't be afraid to ask for help. By arriving early and working independently, I was able to take the time to think things through. It also gave me time to organize the questions that I needed to ask my supervisor each day.

Because I had these questions ready, I was able to talk with my supervisor first thing in the morning before they got busy with their own stuff, run through my questions, and then continue with my work. This increased my competence and grew my independence. I took personal responsibility for my projects and worked on them as if they were my very own.

Leadership lessons . . .

If you look at supervisors who are doing a good job of leading teams, most of the time you'll notice that they start work a little bit earlier than their team members. If you're aspiring to become a supervisor and maybe become a team lead, it's helpful to take on some of those habits that you see in other good supervisors before you get into that position yourself.

Coming into work early to plan your day and spending a little bit of time later to tidy things up for the next day are two habits that manifest from these ideas of responsibility and independence.

I knew I would learn more quickly and be better at my job if I had a little time to get organized and catch my supervisor first thing in the morning. Being aware of what you need to improve allows you to take responsibility for your own development. In doing so, you're owning your weaknesses and asking for help when you need it—an essential element on the road to becoming A Leader Worth Following.

HOW'S YOUR RELATIONSHIP WITH YOUR WORK?

If you're passionate about your job and you're doing work that you believe in, it doesn't really feel like work. In this scenario, you get energy from working, rather than work taking energy from you.

However, especially as you progress in your career, some of the stressors and demands of the job can start to weigh you down, or the job doesn't feel like fun anymore. When that happens, you can begin to resent what you're doing.

You may have been coming to work early, working hard, and exercising these ideas of responsibility and independence. For a time, this has been giving you energy and helping you move along, but one day you show up to do that and you look around and see that other people aren't doing the same. This is when you may start to feel some resentment.

When this happens, there are two things that could be going on. The first is that you're right; other people aren't working as hard as you. The second is that you may have depleted your energy levels. Perhaps other priorities in your life are competing for your time.

We all get that feeling of resentment from time to time, depending on where we are in our careers and our lives. The key is to sit with that feeling and understand it, rather than put that feeling onto external factors. This is a sign for you to spend some time thinking about where you are.

There's a big discussion about work–life balance and what that looks like. I think you need to look at yourself as being in a relationship with your work. If you're in a relationship with another person, especially a serious relationship, it isn't going to be 50-50 all the time. Sometimes relationships are 90-10. Sometimes relationships are 10-90. Sometimes they are 50-50, but they ebb and flow depending on your partner's needs and what else is going on in your lives.

Your relationship with work is the same. Sometimes you're putting a lot into it, whether that's hours or energy—and those two aren't always the same. For me, the idea of work–life balance lies in understanding what priorities you have in your life, as well as at work, and being very, very true to them.

Hopefully, if you can spend some time thinking about those, you can find a way that your best self shows up for your life at work and that you know what you need to do to have your best self for your life when you're not at work. The word *balance* implies that these things have to be even, but I prefer to see it like a flow that shifts depending on what's going on.

Getting this right doesn't mean that you won't have some difficult times if both your personal and professional lives are equally demanding at the same time. When those two things line up, it can be really stressful because you don't feel like there's enough time in the day to deal with everything.

As a leader, you need to understand the ebb and flow of your relationship with your work early on, so that instead of running from any stress you encounter, you're able to understand where it's coming from and therefore deal with it, rather than hiding from it. Often time stress is caused by absolutes that we give ourselves. "I must do this," "I must do that," or "This is the way it has to be" are all examples of either/or think-ing that creates conflict. Life is more complicated than absolutes, so we need to look for balance.

In my experience, it's common for stress to build up when you feel that there's a conflict between your work and personal lives. You feel as though there's not enough time to meet all the needs you have to take care of. By understanding this ebb and flow within the different areas of your life and exploring what this idea of work–life balance really means, you'll be better able to cope with stress, in whatever form that shows up in your life. This is where our next concept, self-awareness, comes in.

A REAL-LIFE STORY: MY FIRST CEO JOB

I mentioned earlier that I started as a transmission design engineer as my first job out of college, and I did that job for two years before my first professional leadership position opened up. I moved from that job after three years to work at a cooperative in Alaska. I worked there for 10 years and progressed in positions and leadership responsibility to the level of chief operating officer, which I held when I left that organiza-tion. I was in my last role as chief executive officer (CEO) of a distribu-tion cooperative for over 20 years. This was my first CEO position, and also my last. 40 years have passed since that day I showed up for work (early) with my bright, shiny engineering diploma and started in that transmission design engineer position.

I have struggled with this idea of work–life balance for these 40 years, and I have made mistakes on both sides of that balance point while I searched for the solution to the equation: Work + Life = Balance. Unfor-tunately, my lived story is not a great example of how to find balance between work and life; it's more a story of what not to do.

It's easy now, as I look back over the past 40 years, to see the times in my life where my balance was off and when the balance was spot-on. It's easy to suggest that it was pressure, stress, someone, or something else that took away my balance. But the truth of the matter is that your balance comes from within you; and you, and you alone, are in charge of you. It is a matter of being true to yourself, but in order to do that you must know what your truths are. In the heat of the moment, we find ourselves being pulled in many directions by so many things and by so many relationships—the relationship with our significant other, the relationships with our family of origin, the relationships with our kids, friends, co-workers, and so on. The truth I have discovered after all these years is that our relationship with ourselves is the first one we need to get right; otherwise, our giving to others, including our jobs, depletes us, creates internal conflicts, anxiety, and ultimately puts our life out of balance.

CHAPTER 4

SELF-AWARENESS

"I believe that self-awareness helps you bring a better version of yourself to work, not just for you, but for the people around you."

There are several elements that fall under the context of self-awareness. However, it's important to understand that if you want to be an effective leader and strive toward becoming A Leader Worth Following, you'll need to be aware of your emotions and how you feel about yourself.

An aspiring Leader Worth Following would do very well to understand how they are feeling about things, but it's an area many people neglect. We can be tone-deaf to our own internal feelings. For a lot of us, it seems as though society teaches us that feelings are bad. We're not supposed to feel mad or angry, hurt or sad. As a result, we tend to stuff those feelings away or act like they're not there until they blow.

Suppressing our feelings works until it doesn't. People are made to feel, and when we shut down feelings that we don't like, we pay the price of shutting down the other feelings as well. Feelings are messy, scary, and complicated, but they give us information if we use the rational part of the brain, our prefrontal cortex, to understand and keep in check that small part of our brain called the amygdala, which is the main source of our emotional response and our fight-or-flight or freeze reaction. If you are under stress, there is a good chance you have a stress hormone called cortisol in your system. It turns out that cortisol actually turns off your rational thinking by inhibiting the functioning of your prefrontal cortex.

However, if you can recognize your feelings and name them, you can remove the power these feelings have over you—whether you're feeling afraid, anxious, or angry—and prevent yourself from experiencing the anxiety these feelings provoke. Recognizing and naming your feelings is the first step to becoming self-aware and developing emotional awareness and control.

We can't control what we don't understand. If you don't know what anxiety is and what that feels like, you may not even realize that you're under stress and feeling anxious. The funny thing is that the people around you, the ones walking on eggshells, feel your mood and your anxiety for you.

In the last chapter, I talked about the idea of Work + Life = Balance, where the two ebb and flow in such a way that you feel balanced. However, when we find ourselves with competing priorities and we're wondering how we can get everything done, we often start to worry. That's when the stress comes in, which is the mental aspect of the situation. The way I look at it is that anxiety is the physical manifestation of that stress in your body. It's that physical feeling in your gut.

The first aspect of self-awareness is being able to identify how you're being affected by particular situations. That's really important, because if you say, "That's a weird feeling, where is this coming from, why is this happening to me?" then you have a chance of being able to bring that into perspective and deal with it. This is you purposefully engaging your rational thinking by turning on your prefrontal cortex to push back the emotional reactions your amygdala is cooking up for you.

This isn't just important for you. If something is bothering you, has upset you, or is really challenging you, it can create negative energy in your body. If you don't know how to deal with that energy, it may end up leaking out onto other people, which can ruin your effectiveness as a leader.

We've all experienced situations where that energy does leak out onto our friends, family, or the people at work; and those are not shining moments of self-leadership. But if you don't know or realize that's what's happening to you, then you don't have much of a chance of resolving it.

EMOTIONAL CONTROL

The idea of emotional control is to sense when you have these feelings and name them. Maybe you're frustrated with somebody and if you're able to say, "I'm feeling frustrated right now," that's a good thing because you have a chance of dealing with it. However, if you're blind to that feeling and don't know what it is, then it can leak out in other ways and affect other people.

The other aspect of emotional control is being able to manage your emotions. You start by understanding that you have feelings and then you use those feelings to diagnose yourself or what might be bothering you. This allows you to figure out a positive way to resolve the situation. That's emotional control: you recognize your feelings about a situation, understand what's driving them, think of the best path forward, and then follow it. When you're able to do this, you'll be seen as a person who is even and predictable.

Of course, if someone never shows any emotion you might wonder about that. But what you're aiming for with your own emotional control is to think about how and when you show your emotions to others. When this is done well, it makes you predictable to others. This is one of the core elements of being A Leader Worth Following, and I believe it's something we should all aspire to. We've all had a boss or coworker that everyone tiptoes around on eggshells because we've been afraid of setting them off. That's not the sign of someone who's predictable and has emotional control.

Having self-awareness of what's going on inside of you and understanding your impact on the people around you is all part of the emotional control you need to develop on your leadership journey. Knowing your impact on others, on your team, and on your organization—and being concerned about that—is a sign of a person who is capable of leading more than just themselves.

Ultimately, I believe that self-awareness helps you bring a better version of yourself to work, not just for you, but for the people around you.

> *"Leaders Worth Following own their weaknesses and know how to ask for help."*

Transitioning from Self-Awareness to Emotional Control

Self-awareness begins with the understanding that you have feelings and that you understand what those feelings are: whether you're mad, happy, sad, or depressed on any given day. The next stage is being able to sit with those feelings and find out where they're coming from. You have to name those feelings and then figure out how you're going to move forward in that moment or that day with those feelings, in a way that's beneficial to you and the people around you. The decision about how you move forward is emotional control.

Now, because we're human, we're not always going to be good at that. We're going to have days when, for whatever reason, we're better at it than others. What we need to do is look at ourselves when we're exercising self-awareness and emotional control and be honest about what we've done well and where we could maybe improve. This ties into the next element of self-awareness, which is self-esteem.

SELF-ESTEEM AKA SELF-LOVE

People who have confidence in their own worth or abilities, even when they make mistakes and are able to forgive themselves for these mistakes, embody high self-esteem. They recognize that they took a particular action and wish they had done better, but then they are able to forgive themselves for what happened, and forgive themselves if they exhibited a lack of emotional control. Another aspect of self-esteem is having the confidence to approach others and make an apology.

Guilt vs. Shame

The difference between guilt and shame is a topic that's often discussed and Brené Brown, in her book *Daring Greatly*,[1] provides a great description of the difference between guilt and shame. Guilt is a feeling, so you know that you did something wrong, whereas shame is the feeling that something is wrong with you. Put simply, it's the difference between: *I did something bad* and *I am bad*.

Having self-esteem allows you to use that feeling of guilt to self-correct and make amends. However, if you don't have adequate self-esteem, those feelings turn to shame and shame does not disclose, it hides. You hide it from yourself, and you certainly hide it from other people.

The concept of self-awareness is ultimately underpinned by this idea of self-esteem, which is to care enough about yourself to forgive yourself for what you did and not let those feelings become shame, which is something you hide and don't talk about. Feelings of shame can really erode the whole process of being self-aware and prevent us from growing as a person and a leader as a result.

---

[1] Brené Brown. (2015). *Daring Greatly: How the Courage to be Vulnerable Transforms the Way We Live, Love, Parent and Lead* (Penguin Life, 2015).

HOW TO DEVELOP YOUR SELF-AWARENESS

First of all, nobody is going to be perfect at this. We'll all have moments where we nail it and are able to self-regulate and come through with an ideal outcome. We'll also have moments where we receive negative outcomes from a situation.

However, if you've noticed you're receiving more negative than positive outcomes from your interactions with others, and you want to make a change, then the first thing you should do is congratulate yourself, because the first step is simply being aware of that desire and making that choice.

When you have this level of self-awareness to think about events and interactions in the context that they work together as a system, you'll have an opportunity to make changes that lead to more positive outcomes.

It's also important to recognize that we all cope with situations differently. For example, the recent Covid-19 pandemic was an external stressor that nobody could run from. Everybody experienced the stress of the pandemic, but we also all experienced it differently.

Part of self-awareness is understanding what you're feeling and how that affects your reactions. But it's also about considering how we handle stress and acknowledging that we all have different mechanisms for coping with it.

There are many techniques out there for calming yourself and becoming more mindful. Being too hungry or too tired are probably the most immediate things that weaken us, so having the self-awareness to recognize when we are super hungry or super tired is important. Personal resilience has a lot to do with how you take care of yourself by making sure you're getting enough rest, participating in physical activity, and eating healthy.

The earlier in your leadership journey you can learn the importance of self-care, the more benefits you will see from it, and I'll talk about the various dimensions of self-care in more detail in Part 4. Being self-aware enough to see how these factors—sleep, physical fitness, and diet—are connected and how they drive outcomes for you is essential, as a leader or an aspiring leader. The sooner you recognize this, the better your journey as A Leader Worth Following will be not only for you, but for the people around you.

Over my life, I've seen lots of examples where people have made unhealthy choices to help them cope with stress, and in the end they paid the price for that.

You can also ask for help and open yourself up to some trusted people in your life or at work. These people will help you by giving you some feedback and encouraging you if you go to them and explain that you want to work on your self-awareness as part of your leadership journey.

WALKING ON EGGSHELLS

When you have someone on a team, either as a team member or a team leader, who is unable to exercise self-awareness and emotional control, the experience for that team is very painful. Often these teams don't function well and there's some discomfort. Depending on how that team is put together, it can get to the point of being very dysfunctional, where people feel like they're walking on eggshells when they're together.

Obviously, every member of the team is there to serve the team and ultimately accomplish the goal, but the dysfunction and walking on eggshells creates a really bad environment.

MIKE'S LEADERSHIP LESSON: DAN, AL, AND HELEN

Dan, Al, and Helen had been working together for months, but unfortunately, there was always an underlying tension between the three of them.

As the engineer leading the project, Dan was always pushing everyone to do more. He was very aware of their deadlines and wanted to make sure the job was done well and on schedule. The deadlines were tight but they were doable if everyone pulled their weight and made a few sacrifices. Dan was so focused on his work and hitting the project deadlines that he didn't stop to think about how his approach might make Al and Helen feel.

Al's specialty was communications, while Helen was a business generalist. Over the course of the project, the two had become friends, a bond largely formed due to Dan's overly pushy approach. The two had been complaining about the way he was pushing the team for months, usually on a coffee break or via a private message or two.

However, as the deadline got closer and Dan pushed ever harder, Helen and Al spent more and more time complaining about how hard he was expecting them to work. "Doesn't he realize there's more to life than work?" Al quipped one day, to which Helen replied, "Clearly his life is his work, otherwise why would he push so hard?"

Tensions were bubbling beneath the surface for weeks, with Al and Helen feeling increasingly marginalized by Dan's approach. In meetings, he didn't seem to care what their opinions were or, at times, even give the illusion of listening to them.

During one particularly stressful phone meeting, where the three of them were trying to fix a specific problem, Al pinged Helen a message, "Do you even think there's any point in us being here? He may as well be talking to two mannequins for all the notice he's taking of us."

"I know! I wonder what the point of having these meetings is when he'll just go off and do what he wants anyway," Helen replied.

"Is it just me, or is his voice sounding even more annoying than usual today?"

"I try to zone it out, treat it like white noise."

"Teach me how! This man has an uncanny ability to make me want to punch a wall!"

"Or him?"... And so the exchange continued, becoming more and more personal.

Dan saw the messages start pinging his phone about 15 minutes into the meeting. Initially he ignored them, but as they became more and more barbed, it rankled him. He put his phone out of sight, tried to continue talking, pretending he hadn't seen them, but they were getting to him.

Eventually he paused: "Al, if you want to punch me I'd rather you came and talked to me about it than sending messages to Helen while we're on a call."

Dead silence met his comment at the other end of the line.

"Punch you . . . ?" stammered Al. "What makes you think I'd want to do that?" he asked hesitantly, although he already knew the answer.

A quick glance at the messages showed him that he'd started his exchange with Helen in the shared group chat, rather than their private chat. Helen, too, was realizing their mistake and cursing under her breath.

Dan ended the meeting with, "I can't talk to the two of you after this, let alone work with you." Of course, he reported the incident to senior management.

After this exchange, it was clear very quickly that mitigation was not an option, so the team was disbanded and new people were assembled to complete the project that Dan, Al, and Helen had started.

Leadership lessons . . .

We can all struggle to get along with our colleagues from time to time, but the way that Al and Helen behaved was inexcusable. In fact, the two of them felt a great deal of embarrassment and shame about their conduct. They knew they had crossed a line in how they were talking, even if the messages hadn't been sent accidentally to Dan.

For his part, Dan was obviously hurt by the comments he saw, but the end result wasn't entirely negative. He had something of an epiphany and realized that he needed to change the way he led and worked. What Al and Helen were unaware of was that Dan was already receiving coaching to help him become less driving and more accommodating to the people on his teams. However, when Dan saw their comments in the group chat, everything he'd been working on became painfully real and seemingly overwhelming.

Do you think all three of these people would have continued to work at the same organization in the long term, even if they were now on separate teams? From my experience of similar incidents, people involved in this kind of issue tend to go their separate ways. They might not all leave at the same time, but being involved in this kind of egregious incident often prompts them to look for work elsewhere.

As an organization, that may mean you lose high-performing, high-potential employees, all due to a lack of self-awareness that creates this kind of dysfunction within a team.

If this is a concern at your organization, how can you prevent similar incidents from happening in the future? My advice is to develop a leadership and training program to help people address these issues and develop their self-awareness to prevent similar situations arising at your firm.

You have to consider how your behavior might affect others you're working with or leading. If you aren't aware, you won't realize there's a problem that needs addressing until it's too late.

ENCOURAGING SELF-AWARENESS AND EMOTIONAL CONTROL

That story is one example of the many things that made us, as an organization, formalize this idea of helping leaders understand what self-leadership looks like, what team leadership looks like, and what organizational leadership looks like. Encouraging people at every level to develop this self-awareness and emotional control involves training, development, and coaching to help them improve, and it means setting out the expectations and outcomes.

There isn't a specific curriculum for self-awareness; however, what we developed was a process for enabling discussions around this topic. It's having conversations about what it takes to become A Leader Worth Following, and talking about what comes up. This is all part of a wider process that involves everyone in the organization talking about issues, challenges, and opportunities.

CHAPTER 5

EVALUATOR/ JUDGMENT

"Critical thinking is developed through experience, learning, and understanding the relationship between things."

In this final chapter of Part 1, we're going to explore critical thinking in the context of leading yourself and leading others. Being able to evaluate situations and make decisions is a crucial part of being a self-leader, as well as a team or organizational leader.

We've already looked at motivators, which are the things that keep you moving in the direction you want to go and remembering what you want. This encompasses the concepts of being dependable, showing up, and being reliable. Then we explored guiding forces, where you take responsibility for things. You see problems or challenges as something of which you can take ownership. You look for places where you can make a change in what you're doing, rather than worrying about what you can't do. You find ways of making progress in the areas you control.

In the last chapter, we looked at self-awareness, which means being aware of your feelings and using them to make decisions about how you're going to interface with yourself and with others to create the most positive outcomes.

Critical thinking begins here, because it relates to you and is the ability to pull all of these things together to make decisions about how you're going to present yourself to your team and your coworkers, as well as make decisions for yourself.

CRITICAL THINKING

At its simplest, critical thinking is being able to synthesize all the information and knowledge that you have into assumptions. You then take those assumptions and make a decision. If you're good at critical thinking, the decisions that you make are generally the right ones. If you're not good at critical thinking, the decisions you make aren't generally the right ones, because the assumptions you made were not the best assumptions.

As I said, critical thinking is the ability to pull your motivators, guiding forces, and self-awareness together, and end up with the best "most right" decisions. This is really important because if you can't get to the best "most right" decisions, leading yourself and leading others is going to be a real challenge. I use the term "most right" decision as a way to emphasize that most complex decisions involve trade-offs. Problems like math problems typically have a correct answer, but as you move more into leadership, many of the decisions you make don't have just one answer. This is where critical thinking comes in.

As a process, critical thinking involves walking through the various data points you have for a particular decision and reaching the best conclusion you can. Critical thinking is developed through experience, learning, and understanding the relationship between things, i.e., "connecting the dots."

A PROCESS OF CONTINUAL LEARNING

Criticial thinking is also a skill that develops over time. Your ability to take all the data and information available to you, and think about what could be the best path forward, improves with experience and growing ability to handle complexity.

For instance, you're in a position where you need to communicate something to people about a particular situation. You have the option to send people an email or pull everybody together on a Zoom call and have a conversation. You choose sending an email over the Zoom call, but the email you send has a different meaning to every person who reads it, because they filter your words based on their perception. At the end of the day, you realize that having a Zoom call would have been a better way to handle it, leading to fewer misunderstandings and confusion.

If you are learning and developing your critical thinking, when you find yourself in that scenario again, you'll analyze the data you have about whether to send an email or hold a video conference, and you'll decide to do a video conference. You've learned from sending that email, which didn't work out well, and you've improved your critical thinking as a result.

As you're leading yourself early in your career, you'll always be working through this process of thinking, "Here's my data and the information I have at hand, here are my assumptions, and here's what I'm going to do." Early in your journey as a leader, your process will be very rigorous. You'll go through these steps every time. You'll learn from those outcomes and the next time it happens, you'll still go through the steps and still get to the decision, but hopefully you'll have learned what leads to better outcomes.

CRITICAL THINKING IS ESSENTIAL FOR LEADERSHIP

Some people haven't learned or can't follow this critical thinking process. Most likely, these people won't find themselves in leadership positions if they can't learn from past mistakes, nor will they have good success in progressing along a leadership journey.

However, those who are good at critical thinking are able to progress more easily on their leadership journey. If you look ahead on the leadership journey to someone who is a very capable and experienced leader, who has led organizations for a long time, you'll find that they don't go through the same rigorous process any more.

That's because our brains work with pattern recognition, and the more experience you get, the more you're able to see patterns in information and situations, and instinctively know what the best "most right" decision is.

I remember going through this process of critical thinking for years in the earlier part of my leadership career and I know it takes mental energy to do that. There are lots of ways you can line up all your assumptions to reach a decision. I was a CEO for over 20 years and I can remember how taxing it was to make decisions and think through situations. I even remember thinking, about five years into my job as CEO, that I would be lucky to last another five years.

Around the 10-year mark, something changed. All of a sudden, this rigor and discipline behind my thinking became much easier; and when I was making decisions, I just knew what to do without having to go through this big process. That was because I had practiced this process and developed these patterns in the way I think about problem solving and decision making.

In self-leadership, you're learning this process of laying everything out to get to decisions and you're learning from the decisions you make. Leaders who are able to move from self-leadership to team leadership have this ability. When you've built a pattern of applying this process and making good decisions, you're ready to move to the next level of leadership.

When you get to team leadership, you have to follow the same process, but the topics are more complex. Because you're leading a team, your decision making isn't just for you any more; it's for all the people in your team too. As you progress from team leadership to organizational leadership, the complexity increases again.

All of this starts by developing your critical thinking as a self-leader. You need to begin here, gain experience, and gradually work up to more complex situations and decision making.

MIKE'S LEADERSHIP LESSON: CARL AND TIM

I've had many leaders throughout my career; some have been good and some have been bad. The worst leader I have ever personally experienced took the job to make his "high five." He came into the job with the idea that he would be served by his job. He was driven to get things done; not for the good of his company, but for his own pride and ego. Carl wouldn't take the time to sit with the resistance he might be feeling from others; instead, he would lash out, personalize everything, and assume the victim role. Carl would drink, tell people off, and then apologize the next day. He was unpredictable and had no clue of his impact on others. He saw the organization and its people as being of service to him. In the end, he left a large amount of organizational carnage in his wake which took years to work through.

By contrast, I had another leader named Tim who had very high emotional intelligence. Tim could read people as well as be analytical. He used his feelings, or his gut, and his intellect to make decisions. Tim was the consummate negotiator and was able to renegotiate seemingly ironclad contracts with large corporations that had no incentive or reason to renegotiate. His skills saved his company millions in excessive costs and changed the "old way" of doing business. Kenny Rogers's song titled *The Gambler* has a famous refrain: "You have to know when to hold 'em, know when to fold 'em, know when to walk away, know when to run." This is a great real-life example of emotional control, self-awareness, and critical thinking. Tim was an example of what it looks like to be striving to become A Leader Worth Following.

Leadership Lessons . . .

What I learned from Carl, the bad leader, was the importance of sitting with your discomfort in order to understand what it may be trying to teach you. Good leaders will sleep on difficult decisions, rather than behaving rashly and having to apologize the next day. The wake that a bad leader leaves is something the organization pays for—sometimes for a long time.

What I learned from Tim was that good leaders, and Leaders Worth Following, trust their guts and their minds. He also showed me the value of emotional intelligence in a leadership role. Understanding others is important, but you have to first understand yourself.

It's really easy to project your feelings of worry, anxiety, fear, and uncertainty onto other people, especially if you aren't spending the time to understand yourself. Being able to understand others is critical for good leadership, yet the challenge is that you have to understand yourself first. Your ability to think and process external information relies on your ability to understand yourself.

As a leader, you have to be able to see past your own ego to understand and empathize with others; otherwise, you are likely to make poor decisions and hurt people along the way. You need to understand your emotions and analyze them to ensure you're emotionally predictable for those around you, and that you make the best decisions you can in any given situation.

HOW TO DEVELOP YOUR CRITICAL THINKING SKILLS

To develop your critical thinking skills, begin with an understanding of the concept of connecting everything to make a decision. I think it's very helpful to make your process visual and, in my experience, we tend to do this instinctively by making lists or mind maps. Mind maps are a particularly easy way to visualize your decision-making process, showing how things link together and lead to outcomes.

Collaborating with other people is also useful for developing your critical thinking. Getting everyone in a room together (or an online meeting space these days) and whiteboarding a particular issue, walking through the scenarios, is really important. Using whiteboards, either in person or virtually, is a good process for collaborative decision making. As a self-leader, you can collaborate with coworkers whom you know and trust. You might start by following this process yourself, and then bring in just one coworker for advice or additional input.

Hopefully, if you're in an organization that understands the process of developing leaders, your supervisor or team leader will be running collaborative decision-making sessions like this frequently, and you'll see that model and recognize it for the opportunity that it is.

Even without intention, this often happens to varying degrees in any organization because it's just the way humans work together. If you're aware of this, you can tune into those situations and recognize them as opportunities to develop your critical thinking.

THE BUILDING BLOCKS FOR SELF-MANAGEMENT AND SELF-FOCUS

All four of the aspects that we've talked about as part of self-management—the motivators, the guiding forces, self-awareness, and the evaluator—are independent, but they work together to position you to become a really good self-leader and a really great coworker. Becoming good at applying these in your everyday work life positions you to take the next steps on your leadership journey and gives you a strong foundation from which to develop as A Leader Worth Following.

This means moving into leading teams and applying the same skills, but maybe applying them to different situations and to challenges and opportunities with increased complexity.

Now that you've made it through the ideas and concepts of being a great self-leader and a great team member, it's time to focus on scaling up and looking at them from multiple directions and perspectives, and understanding what it's going to take to become a great leader of teams, one who people are happy and excited to follow.

INTERPERSONAL ABILITY/ TEAM FOCUS

As you move from self-leadership to leading teams, your interpersonal ability becomes more important. This is about your awareness of your effect on the people around you and your ability to motivate and inspire others to focus their efforts on what the team is trying to accomplish.

There are many ways to look at interpersonal ability and a person's ability to influence others. Someone could be very passionate about a topic or a goal and by sharing their passion they inspire others to feel that passion. Some people just have that natural charisma and others are drawn to their energy and want to be part of it.

However you view interpersonal ability, the big step is recognizing it in yourself. If you're observing and developing leaders, then it's also recognizing the people who can bring the energy of others and their focus to bear on goals that will be best accomplished through a team effort.

In the first part of this book, we explored self-leadership. When you're working on self-leadership, your goals, tasks, and everything you're doing is very specific. However, as you start to move into team leadership, the complexity of the challenges and goals that you're working on become more than one person can do.

This is why you need to understand the importance of teams. You'll need to leverage different expertise and different perspectives on problems or challenges to accomplish goals. Your ability to lead in these more complex situations all begins with your ability to work well with others and to lead teams.

>>>>>>>>>>>>>>>>>>>>>>>>>>>>>>>>>>>>

CHAPTER 6

UNDERSTANDING YOUR WAKE

"It's really important to understand what it's like for people to be led by you, and to understand what effect you have on other people."

When I talk about understanding your wake, I find the easiest analogy to describe it is that of a boat. Imagine that you're driving a boat across a calm lake. As you move through the water, the engine creates a wake. How big and how turbulent that is will depend on how fast you're going and the way in which you're handling the boat.

Now imagine that someone is trying to water-ski behind your boat. If your wake is too turbulent, that's going to be very challenging for them. You can also see that the ripples of your wake reach much further than just the water behind your boat, as I explained in Chapter 2.

We all have a wake, but when you're aware of it and understand it, hopefully you'll look back and won't see chaos behind you.

MIKE'S LEADERSHIP LESSON: GEORGE BUSH (AND BROCCOLI)

"I do not like broccoli. And I haven't liked it since I was a little kid and my mother made me eat it. And I'm president of the United States, and I'm not going to eat any more broccoli!"[1]

Those words, spoken by George H. W. Bush during his presidency, had a stronger effect than he likely imagined. By talking negatively about broccoli, he created a huge dent in the industry. People even stopped eating broccoli because the president had said he didn't like it. All the broccoli producers were upset because he was hurting their business.

This might be a story that you've heard before, but maybe not. Either way, it includes some important lessons around being aware of your wake.

Leadership Lessons . . .

If you don't see your wake and how it affects other people, then you won't be sensitive to those "broccoli" moments you might have as a leader.

As a leader, people will be more willing to give you the discretionary effort you need to help your company be successful if they feel as though you see them and are aware of how your actions affect them. They will meet you with their best energy and their best selves to work to overcome challenges in the

---

[1] George H. W. Bush "I'm President, So No More Broccoli!" *New York Times*, March 23, 1990. https://www.nytimes.com/1990/03/23/us/i-m-president-so-no-more-broccoli.html.

organization. Encouraging this effort involves taking a more egalitarian approach to leadership where you don't always have to be the best at everything, you don't have to make the most money, and you don't need to have the best parking spot.

You have to acknowledge your gaps in knowledge and ask for help filling them. Over the years, I've watched ego take people down because they couldn't admit they were wrong, or they made a bad decision and blamed it on someone else. These aren't the actions of A Leader Worth Following.

Instead, you have to look at how you can change yourself first before asking others to do the same. Sometimes that change might come in the form of taking a pay cut alongside the rest of your staff. I know making such a decision is rare. How often do you see leaders of struggling organizations letting everyone else take pay cuts while they still take home a large salary and bonuses? It's particularly endemic in bankruptcies, where the executives' bonus plans somehow seem to survive the bankruptcy. If you look at most bankruptcies, you'll typically find an article somewhere about how the top leadership is still getting paid big money while everyone else in the company is suffering.

If you truly aspire to become A Leader Worth Following, you have to lead from the front. You have to be willing to change yourself first, take responsibility, and own your weaknesses or mistakes.

When you fail to consider your wake as a leader, you will leave turmoil and carnage behind you. You have to think carefully about whether your actions or words could have a negative impact on others. If the answer is "yes," consider how you can change your actions or words to, at the very least, minimize that negative impact.

As a leader, it's important to understand what it's like for people to be led by you, and to understand what effect you have on other people. The first stage lies with the understanding that you do have an effect on those around you. However, you need to take this further and make sure that the people you lead will find it easy to follow you.

There are several areas that you can develop to understand your wake, and we're going to talk about the three most important of these in this chapter: objectivity, listening, and being sensitive to others.

> *"Leaders Worth Following have great expectations and an even greater heart."*

OBJECTIVITY

Objectivity begins with keeping an open mind. When you're beginning to lead teams, you'll be bringing other people's expertise and experiences to bear on solving a problem or accomplishing a goal. To do this, you have to be objective. If, however, you've already decided what needs to happen and where things are going, then you haven't left any room for the people around you to contribute and take ownership of the situation.

Obviously, we all have thoughts and opinions on where things need to go and how they should be done. That's OK, but where you can get into trouble as a leader, especially when your leadership is formally recognized, is when you're in a situation where it feels like everybody in the room is waiting for you to tell them what to do or make a decision about how things should proceed.

In some situations, this approach can work well, provided you're familiar with what's going on. However, the problem that you run into when you lead in this way is that your team's work and output will only be as good as you. That may work for a while but as you get better at leading teams, you'll be assigned more and more complex problems. This is when objectivity becomes crucial.

At this point, there is a strong need for you, as the leader, to be objective. You have to suspend your thoughts, desires, and opinions and invite other people to contribute and give their perspectives. To me, this is objectivity in leadership: putting aside your thoughts and opinions on how to solve a problem and getting feedback from your team.

When you listen to your team's thoughts and opinions, not only will it help them feel more engaged and make them want to contribute more to what's going on, but it will also improve the results you get. My experience has shown that when you're able to take that step back and adopt objectivity, the results are much greater than if you just tell people what to do.

As a newly appointed leader or supervisor, there might be a temptation to do things your way and while you can do that, this is a short-sighted approach to take. Ultimately, your role as a team leader is to bring that team together cohesively in order to identify and solve a problem or complete the task at hand.

The majority of the time, I think it's important for the leader to set aside their own ideas and get feedback from team members. However, urgent situations, or perhaps a crisis, requires the leader to take an immediate and direct approach. Or, if your team members are relatively inexperienced, you may need to be more direct as a leader.

Even if this is the case, there is a saying that is worth remembering: "If you want to learn how *not* to do something, call an expert." The value of a team doesn't just lie in their experience. The value of a beginner's mind is important in problem solving too. When you can be objective and give everyone the opportunity to share their feedback, you'll likely find some good ideas because the people in your team may not have convinced themselves that the problem can't be solved in a certain way. As much as you're willing to teach your team, you're also willing to learn from them.

A Leader Worth Following cultivates a mindset of objectivity, suspending their thoughts and inclinations to make room for others to contribute. This is closely linked with the next area we're going to explore: listening.

LISTENING

When a leader has that objectivity mindset, which means they keep an open mind, they are truly willing to hear what other people have to say and to take that to heart. This mindset is internal, but the external way to show objectivity to people is by really listening to them.

I think we've all been in meetings where we're talking to somebody and it's obvious that their focus is someplace else. I've certainly been in meetings where we've had a team assembled to work on solving a problem or a challenge, so there's some dialogue happening; but when you look around you realize that some people are focused on something else, such as looking at their phone or typing an email. Some of that might be relevant to what's going on, but more often it's a sign that they aren't actively listening.

If you're going to listen to people as a leader, you need to be present to them, whether you're listening in a group or one-on-one. The ability to be a good listener is essential for leading teams and for becoming A Leader Worth Following.

MIKE'S LEADERSHIP LESSON: THE IMPORTANCE OF LISTENING

"Hi Mike, what's going on? What's the problem?" Paul barely looked up from the mountain of paperwork in front of him and continued writing as I was speaking. I continued talking, noticing that he wasn't taking notes about what I was saying but that he was doing his paperwork. I paused, and he looked up at me over his glasses and said, "You don't mind if I sign this paperwork while you're talking, do you?"

"Of course not." What else could I say? This interaction happened early in my career. Paul was my supervisor and I'd gone to talk to him about a challenge I was having. In that situation, it's a bad question because most people aren't going to tell off their supervisor. (I certainly didn't.) I kept talking, but I was aware he wasn't really hearing what I was saying.

Leadership Lessons . . .

The thing my supervisor should have done in that situation was to set down his pen and listen to me talk about my problem. But in asking me that leading question, he was banking on my politeness and knew that with the power differential between us, I wouldn't say, "Yes, I mind."

However, I would say that someone who has the courage to ask their supervisor to put down their pen is probably someone worth listening to.

I'd also like to add that I believe taking notes when you're listening to someone is important. Jotting things down that are related to what they're saying can help you show people that you're actually listening to them. But in this case, my supervisor was working on something completely different and didn't have his full attention on me.

Listening is about keeping yourself fully engaged. As the receiver of information, there are lots of ways you can do that and taking some really quick notes and jotting your thoughts down is just one of them.

You have to think about the other person and how they will feel in all your interactions as a leader. When you only consider yourself, you're letting your ego take over and you aren't demonstrating that you're willing to learn from others. If you truly want to become A Leader Worth Following, you need to empathize with others and you can only do that effectively if you truly listen to them.

ACTIVE LISTENING SKILLS

Most of us understand basic active listening skills, but as a leader it's important to make sure you're using them with your team. They can involve paraphrasing what the other person is saying to you, so that they are hearing that you've understood them. Restating ideas or points back to them can be helpful too. Asking questions to clarify points is another important element of active listening.

But I think the most important one is to look at people and make eye contact with them while they're speaking. Your body language is also really important, because when your body language is consistent with theirs, it demonstrates that you're really listening. This doesn't have to be complicated; it's simply a case of mirroring how they're positioning the parts of their body, whether that's crossing their arms or clasping their hands together.

Mirroring someone's body language creates a sense of comfort for the person speaking and invites them into a deeper conversation because it shows that you're paying attention.

Some body language all of us understand. For instance, if you start talking to someone and they cross their arms and close themselves off, you're going to get the sense that they really don't want to listen to you.

Another tip to show someone that you're really listening to them is to physically show that you're putting aside what you're currently doing in order to pay attention to them. If you have an office, that could be coming out from behind your desk and sitting at a conference table with them. It might be as simple as closing your laptop or turning off your computer so that you can be more present with that person. This whole concept of active listening is about finding ways that you can reduce the barriers between you and the other person as they try to talk and as you try to listen.

I've found active listening to be such a powerful concept for leaders to grasp that I've included a chapter about it in Part 4 of this book. Active listening has the power to not only improve your relationships with others, but to help you grow and develop personally and professionally. It's an essential tool for any Leader Worth Following to possess.

COMMUNICATING IN A VIRTUAL WORLD

With the Covid-19 pandemic and the rapid change to more virtual working environments, leaders have had to adapt quickly. One thing I noticed among my team leads during this time was that the ones who are really instinctive and natural leaders very quickly increased the frequency with which they were communicating with everyone on their teams.

Before the pandemic, they would maybe have a longer weekly conversation with each person to check in, or a face-to-face chat every couple of days. But in the virtual world, they quickly made the effort to have a face-to-face call with their folks twice a day. These were just short conversations throughout the day, but they were quite effective as a way to keep connected to their people, as well as make themselves available.

Leaders also need to be aware of the signals that they might be sending to their team about their willingness to listen and be available in a virtual environment. A lot of the software that we use allows us to see whether the other person is busy before we call them because we can see their calendar. However, I'm not sure that's such a great idea because it puts up a barrier that might prevent people from reaching out to you.

It might help to consider this as your virtual wake. When you set up calendar items where you're "busy" and your diary is full of appointments and "red" blocks of time, it can give the appearance that you're not available for your team. When you're collaborating virtually, it's important to be aware of what kind of signals you're sending about your availability and willingness to visit with your team. This links with the final point related to understanding your wake: being sensitive to others.

BEING SENSITIVE TO OTHERS

Sensitivity as a leader is your ability to understand how your people are feeling, and it helps you to develop empathy with them. I think a lot of people confuse empathy and sympathy. Brené Brown describes the difference between empathy and sympathy with a story about someone falling down a well.

You fall into a well and you're trapped at the bottom. The person who has sympathy for you looks over the top of the well and says, "Man you're in a well, that really sucks, that's not good." The person who has empathy for you jumps into the well to keep you company and supports you as you find your way out.[1]

When it comes to sensitivity to others, Leaders Worth Following need to meet people where they are and understand what they're going through. So when people come to you as a leader, with problems or challenges, don't be afraid to feel what they're feeling and join them in their struggle, whether that's frustration at work or challenges in their personal lives.

We all try to bring our best selves to work, but the reality is that when you come to work you bring everything with you. That means if you're having a bad day at home, you're potentially going to be having a bad day at work. It also means that if you have a bad day at work, you may have a bad evening at home when you leave. Even though we try to keep these things separate, we don't always succeed.

As a leader you need to be able to understand what other people are going through, whether that's things that are going on in their own lives or, in the context of understanding your wake, understanding how your behavior affects others.

If you're doing things that are making people uncomfortable and you're totally blind to that, you're probably not going to get very far as a leader of teams. Having awareness of how other people are feeling and understanding people's emotions are essential if you want to move on from leading a team to leading multiple teams within an organization.

---

[1] Brené Brown, *Brené Brown on Empathy*, RSA, December 10, 2013, https://www.thersa.org/video/shorts/2013/12/brene-brown-on-empathy.

Having an ability to understand people's emotions and where they're coming from is the mark of an authentic leader.

UNDERSTANDING YOUR WAKE

Understanding your wake and your effect on others means that you're prepared to look behind your speedboat and see what your wake is doing.

If you don't have objectivity and aren't willing to accept that other people's ideas might be good too; if you don't have the capacity to listen to people; and if you're not sensitive to the outcome of situations or your effect on them, their effect on each other, and the effect that has on getting the job done, then you're the guy in the speedboat who's driving too fast, creating a huge wake and knocking people over.

You never look back and you think life is great, but if you just took a moment to look behind you then you'd see the havoc that you're creating. Failing to pay attention to, and understanding your wake is the risk you take if you don't develop a mindset of objectivity, actively listen to people, and display sensitivity for others.

> *"Leaders must understand what it feels like to live in their wake."*

In the long term, it's much easier if you're aware of the wake that you leave behind. In order to do that, you need to embody the qualities I've talked about in this chapter. Be objective, listen to others, and care about how others feel. Be aware of what's going on with other people each day, as well as how they're being affected by what you're asking them to do and how you're asking them to do it.

I can tell you that there was a time in my career when I didn't care about my wake very much at all. Early on, I was very much results driven. I knew these things were important, but I approached them as a box-ticking exercise instead of fully embracing them. I would give someone my five minutes of listening and check that box.

Checking the box is better than not even knowing that box is there to be checked, but being A Leader Worth Following is about far more than simply checking a box. Internalizing these things is what gives leaders and teams resiliency and sustainability, which is why objectivity, active listening, and sensitivity to others are so important.

CHAPTER 7

TEAM BUILDING

"Communication underpins everything on your teams, but it also underpins the success of a business."

Whether you're building teams for the short or long duration, it's something you really have to get right. If you're on a good team everybody knows it, and you can feel it. Similarly, if you're part of a not-so-good team, everybody knows it too. Entire volumes have been written on teams and team building, and what's contained in this book is far from exhaustive. This chapter discusses a few guiding principles to help you as you get used to building and working with teams.

Without those principles and best practices, teams can form in a haphazard way. As you move further along your journey towards becoming A Leader Worth Following, it's important to be deliberate in how you build teams. This helps ensure the team functions well and saves a lot of wasted time and energy.

The first of the principles I'd like to introduce you to is team chartering.

TEAM CHARTERING

Team chartering is setting out a written framework for how your team functions. This is actually the start of the team-building process, because everyone works together to build the charter. Charters can be formal or informal, depending on the lifespan of the team. If you're in a team that will be together in the long term, your charter may be a document that you'll look at periodically, such as every year. If you're putting together an ad hoc team, your charter may look completely different. No matter what kind of charter you're creating, it's the process and functions that you need to go through that are important.

HOW TO CREATE A TEAM CHARTER

Whether for a long- or short-term team, the first step towards creating a team charter is for everybody on that team to know its purpose. That might sound like I'm stating the obvious, but when you want to create alignment with people, sometimes stating the obvious is important.

That general purpose may be established by those higher up in the organization, but as the team talks about what they're responsible for, it can become very specific. I believe this is an important part of starting to build a team and bringing people together. Their first deliverable as a team is to create this charter, which sets out the team's purpose and gives them guidelines for how they will work together.

This includes how the team will communicate with each other, such as email, video, telephone, or face-to-face. At this stage, you can make sure that everybody is comfortable with the type of communication the team chooses. It's helpful for everybody to talk openly about communication, and this also means you can discuss resolving conflicts and how you'll handle that within the team too.

You also set out how the team makes decisions. Is it a consensus-type decision? Is there a formal vote? Do you all talk about things together and give everyone a chance to share their input, but the team leader decides? You can really dig into your decision-making processes.

Part of creating your team charter also involves setting out norms and expectations for team members. One of the easy examples here is being on time for your meetings. Another expectation to consider, especially nowadays given that we all work digitally, is multitasking and, specifically, what level of multitasking is acceptable during a meeting.

For example, most of our resources these days are stored in the cloud and people may use notetaking apps. When you're in a meeting and see someone looking at their screen, you want to know that they haven't gotten distracted by something unrelated to the meeting topic. Setting out these expectations and guidelines ahead of time means that, instead of wondering whether someone is actually paying attention, you can take it as a given that they'll be looking at their screen only if it relates to what you're talking about, such as taking notes for later use.

When I was at PRECorp, we discovered how important it was to lay out some structure and framework for our teams about 10 years before I stepped down as CEO. In my experience, the higher-performing teams, in terms of the ones that perform well together, have identified this idea of team chartering either deliberately or accidentally. When a team knows its purpose and has clear rules of engagement, and everybody honors those and moves forward with them, the team is able to work much more effectively.

The final element of chartering relates to the expectation of how long a team will last. When you put your team together, you want everybody to have a sense of how long it will last. This will enable you to decommission that team and recognize their work when they have completed it. You don't want the team to just quietly die. You want to have a deliberate dissolution of the team, and almost make it an event, so there's a deliberate beginning and a deliberate ending to the people on your team coming together.

Overcoming Resistance to the Concept of Team Charters

When you're introducing the concept of team charters, you might encounter some resistance. Whenever you do anything that's a change, there is likely to be some form of resistance, depending on the culture of the people around you and their experience within teams.

Leading people through change is part of your job as a leader. So, putting a team together, creating a charter, and having those discussions is, in itself, a learning process in how to build and lead teams. It's a great opportunity! Once people have been through this process and worked within a team that has a charter, they become supportive of the process and feel as though something is missing if this doesn't happen when a new team comes together.

It's never too late to go through this process. If you have a team whose members aren't working well together, it can definitely be recovered. To do that requires you, as leader, to show your vulnerability. When there is dysfunction in a team, everybody knows it and no one wants to talk about it, so having the courage to step up and state the obvious is the first step in this process. Perhaps acknowledge that you could have taken a better approach to forming the team, talk about how you want to change as a leader, and then take the discussion from there.

Returning to Your Charter

When you have a long-standing team, such as an executive staff team for a company, members are going to come on and off that team. People and situations change over time. When I was at PRECorp, the executive staff team, at times, found ourselves in the position where we didn't feel as though our meetings were going right. It felt as though there was grit in the gears, and things didn't seem to be flowing.

A lot of the time, that's a sign that it's time to revisit your charter. When you look at it again, you might realize that you don't do this anymore, or that the situation has changed and certain elements aren't working anymore. This is a cue to figure out a new way of approaching things.

This was particularly evident when I wrote *The No-Os of Leadership* shortly after the Covid-19 pandemic and the big change in the way we interacted socially that came with it. I think the teams that worked well together at this time were able to take this process and jumpstart it to look at the team in the context of where everybody currently was. The teams that did this were typically functioning much better than the teams that were simply wondering why things didn't work anymore.

MIKE'S LEADERSHIP LESSON: LIGHTBULB MOMENT

One of my biggest lightbulb moments in relation to team building came when I was working in GCU's Ken Blanchard Executive MBA program.

Ken Blanchard is a world-famous author, and his first big impact in the business world was a book called *One Minute Manager.* In his MBA program, he shares his model for high-performing teams. I was completing this MBA program when I was CEO, and one of the great things about my experience in that program was that I was developing my leadership and bringing my learnings back to work—which meant that my executive staff were pretty much going through the program with me. I didn't realize it at the time, but I was exhibiting a willingness to teach, a core element of becoming A Leader Worth Following.

As I was learning and we were implementing what I had learned, I'd talk to my executive staff about what we were doing and what was coming next. At first, we would chat and laugh about it, but as time went on we were implementing things that made the company and the team better.

The idea of a team charter came from this program, and it was a totally new concept for the company and the people working there. We started with it at the executive staff level. I wouldn't say we were a high-functioning team back then.

There were lots of internal conflicts within the team. We had many of the typical components of dysfunction within a team in that we had lots of silos where people were just concerned with their own little world. We had overt conflict between team members, where the conflict was face-to-face, and we had behind-the-scenes conflict. The style in which the team was run meant that not everybody felt able to contribute to conversations, which had the effect of some team members feeling like they were on the sidelines, even though they weren't.

Unfortunately, we had pretty much all of those elements happening in our senior team, but as we learned how to build a high-performing team following the Ken Blanchard model, the executive staff began to come together and were much more cohesive and focused. We still had conflict, but it was managed in a constructive way.

Leadership Lessons . . .

Conflict within teams is actually good, because you want to have those differing opinions within your team, and you want people who are passionate about their ideas. However, if you don't have structure and an accepted way for that conflict to manifest, be discussed, and be resolved, it can cause issues.

In this scenario, conflict creates hurt feelings within your team. It can create animosity. One of the most important things that a team charter does is put all this on the table and allows everyone to have a dispassionate conversation about things that people feel very passionate about.

Once you reach a resolution, your team begins to function much better than it did before. That's especially true in the case of executive staff or leadership teams. If those high-level teams are in conflict, everybody knows it, not only the people in the team but also those around them.

This comes back to the concept of understanding your wake that I talked about in the last chapter. You have a team wake as well as a personal one, and if your team isn't functioning properly, it will leave a big wake behind it that will affect even more people within your organization.

The benefit of being deliberate in team building, introducing a chartering process, and bringing people within teams together with an openness to discuss issues is that you reduce this negative, disruptive wake. The sooner you can bring these conflicts and issues out into the open and get people talking about them, the sooner that team will shift to becoming a high-performing team.

Being able to see how your way of working and the decisions you're making are affecting others is crucial for strong leaders and strong leadership teams. It helps every member of that leadership team make further progress towards becoming A Leader Worth Following themselves.

OPENNESS

Openness in this context is people being willing to talk about what's going on within their team and how things are functioning. This is about being honest and facing the reality of the situations in which you and your team find yourselves.

I believe that there can never be too much openness when it comes to how a team is functioning, how the members of the team relate to each other, and what is affecting the team. The only time that openness could possibly become an issue is in the sense of off-topic oversharing, where people share things that have nothing to do with the team.

When this happens, it's important to take things "offline." We've actually found that the team chartering process really helps with this because it allows you as the leader to step in and do just that.

For example, maybe the team is having a dialogue and an issue comes up that's affecting the team, but after talking about it for a few minutes it becomes quite obvious that the issue isn't really a team issue. Perhaps one or two people have a few things they need to straighten out between themselves. Within your team chartering process, you can identify a way that's acceptable to take these issues "offline."

What I mean by taking things offline is that, if you're having a team meeting and two people are having a conversation within that meeting to the point that the rest of the team become bystanders to the discussion, anyone in the team can just say, "Hey, can you guys take this offline?" It's a way to pause the discussion and allow those two people to continue their conversation outside the meeting. They can then bring anything that's relevant to the wider team to the next meeting.

Openness is important in enabling this to happen. We should understand that sometimes some dialogues aren't relevant for the entire team. Taking it offline is a mechanism to pull that dialogue out of the team environment and let people deal with whatever situations or challenges they're facing without affecting the rest of the team.

COMMUNICATION

Communication is one of the most important aspects to focus on as A Leader Worth Following. Essentially, communication is two things: it's conveying information, but it's also being willing to hear and absorb information.

We introduced employee opinion surveys at PRECorp about 15 years before I stepped down as CEO. When I retired from that role, we had around 100 questions in the survey and would typically see about 95% of our employees complete the survey every year. The survey talked about leadership, communication, people's alignment with the company's strategy, and their understanding of what was going on—it was a very comprehensive survey. When you looked back at the surveys year after year, and you looked at the various challenges that manifested in different areas of the company, they always came back to communication.

> *"A leader has to face reality. You can't fix a problem that you don't know you have."*

I don't believe that there's a solution to a problem that can't be enhanced by communication. At the same time, it doesn't matter how good something is: if you don't have good communication, you run the risk of something good turning out poorly. Over the years I have learned that one of my biggest mistakes in communicating is thinking that I clearly expressed myself, but others didn't grasp what I was telling them at all.

Communication underpins everything on your teams, but it also underpins the success of a business. An organization is a series of teams that are working together, which makes communication in relation to teams particularly important.

I've already touched on the importance of discussing the different channels of communication that your team will use. Different types of communication may work better in different scenarios. For example, email might be the preferred method of communication to get information sent out; but if you have a problem or challenge and need to brainstorm, in our organization, the preference was always for a call for a face-to-face meeting. (Obviously after Covid-19 that changed, and we all adapted to using online tools such as Zoom and Teams to have those more intensive problem-solving or brainstorming sessions.)

How you communicate within your team and which mode of communication you use for different purposes is just the first layer of communication you have to consider. You also need to think about how one team communicates with other teams within the company to explain what they've done and where things are. It's not only communication within the team that needs to be deliberate, but also communication outside the team.

There has to be a deliberate process for communicating outside of your team. For example, after a meeting, we would always check in by answering the following questions:

▸ What do we need to communicate to our stakeholders about this meeting?

▸ How are we going to communicate that?

▸ When is this communication going to come out?

It's important to understand that every team has an external effect, whether that's on other teams within an organization or on external stakeholders. For teams to function well, and for organizations (which are a collection of teams working together) to function well, there needs to be agreement about what is being communicated by teams, who that's being communicated to, and how that process will work.

MIKE'S LEADERSHIP LESSON: COVID MISCOMMUNICATION

From time to time, miscommunication can happen within any organization, and I'd like to share a story about how to deal with that as a leader, whether it was your miscommunication or someone else's.

At PRECorp, I liked to do periodic updates to the team. Especially during 2020–21, these updates were every two to three weeks. I put out formal video communications to help people deal with and manage their own anxiety as it related to the Covid-19 situation.

Before I did these videos, I would talk to my executive staff and we agreed on the high points that needed to be updated. I would then turn that into a dialogue with the team that we held over Zoom. When I was finished with the video meeting, a recording was sent out to everyone so if they couldn't make the meeting, they could watch it, and anyone who was there had the recording to refer to if they wanted. As well as sending out the recording, we also followed up with a newsflash, which was a brief email sent to everyone in the company that provided a quick synopsis of what was said.

Not long before my retirement, we discussed a procedure that we needed to implement pretty quickly because it related to Covid personal protection. In the meeting, I verbally told everybody the safety procedures: If you're going to be at your desk, don't wear a mask. If you're going to be away from your desk and walking around the building, wear a mask. If you're going to be in a meeting where you can't socially distance, wear a mask.

When the summary email of the meeting was sent out, it said: *CEO Mike Easley strongly suggests wearing masks.*

I saw that and thought, "That's not what I said. It wasn't a suggestion." My first reaction was to want to find out how my instructions had been misunderstood. Often when something like this happens, the first reaction is to pick up the phone or send an email in frustration to the person who got the communication wrong.

But that wasn't what I did. Instead, I called the VP of that division and said, "Hey, did you see the newsflash that came out summarizing the meeting about the use of masks?" They said, "Yes." So I asked, "Could you look at that again and make sure my message was right on that?" The VP looked at the communication again, realized that wasn't what was said in the meeting, and a correction was sent out within half an hour.

This isn't the end of the story though. We all know that people tend to take information and hear what they want to hear. A lot of times, corrections don't sink in or people simply miss them.

I gave another video update about mask procedure. What I didn't do was say, "In case you didn't hear me last time, this is what I said . . ." Instead, I said, "I've been thinking about this a long time, and I think I could just be a little clearer about what I meant. I've learned some things and I've thought about it . . ." And then I said the same thing that I said two weeks before, but in a way that didn't threaten people.

Leadership Lessons . . .

Instead of rushing to yell at somebody who made a mistake, I took a step back and approached it from a wider perspective. I asked the question, "I'm curious to know, did I get this right? Could you look at this for me and give me a sanity check on what we're saying here?"

Rather than throwing stones at someone or laying blame, I corrected the miscommunication gently. This isn't only for the benefit of the person who sent the original miscommunication. Some people may have been thinking differently about the situation, or they may have read the first article but not seen the correction. I don't want to throw all of those people under a bus.

When there is miscommunication, I think leaders do well to not cast stones at the people who miscommunicated. As leaders, we always have to take the extra time to not lay blame on people, to accept responsibility, and then come to it again to try and fix it without throwing people under the bus.

You have to be confident in your leadership style to be able to do that, even though the situation may or may not be your fault. Blaming somebody for a mistake that was made and then setting yourself up as the savior of the day isn't what leadership is. The person who made the mistake knows it and they feel it.

If, as a leader, you accept responsibility for mistakes and not cast them on somebody else, that person will remember that, which builds loyalty and encourages them to do even better next time. This is how you become A Leader Worth Following. Personally, I think that works well for organizations. I can certainly say that it worked well in ours.

By thinking about how someone else will feel when they've made a mistake, you can approach the situation from a place of empathy where not only do you correct the mistake, but everyone feels good about the outcome.

CHAPTER 8

SHAPING A TEAM

"As you're growing and developing your team, you're also growing and developing yourself."

As you move further along your leadership journey, and especially as you reach the executive level, you should always be trying to grow and develop your team. Leading is an evolutionary process. As you're growing and developing your team, you're also growing and developing yourself. As I said at the beginning of this book, becoming A Leader Worth Following is a journey, not a destination. If you're ever satisfied that you're the leader that you want to be, you're probably not the leader you should be.

"Leaders need to develop a keen sense of empathy for those they lead."

A critical aspect of being a leader is knowing when somebody within your team needs to find another team to be on. It's all too easy to hide from team conflicts when somebody needs to move on.

In this situation, everybody on the team knows there's a conflict, but rarely is anyone talking about it. It's the proverbial "elephant in the room" that everyone tiptoes around. As a leader, you can't avoid this conflict forever.

MIKE'S LEADERSHIP LESSON: GETTING THE CEO JOB

The first time I experienced this situation was when I joined PRECorp 20 years ago. This was my first CEO position, and the environment I came into was one of extreme dysfunction. The acting CEO had interviewed for the job and didn't get it. He was the manager of engineering and operations, and in his time as acting CEO, he had essentially restructured the company assuming that he would get the job.

He had built the team around him, and when I came in as CEO, he wasn't happy at all. But the issues went beyond just this one person. The whole mentality of the team was one where people weren't used to making decisions for themselves. They were used to being told what to do.

The whole hierarchy of the company was built around what I'd describe as a "command and control" model, which meant that everybody was only as good as the person who was in front of them.

When I came on board, I had this guy who was angry about not getting the CEO job and a company operating on a structure that I considered to be dysfunctional. It was a challenging environment to come into, especially as someone who had never been a CEO before.

When you first come into a team, you have to build trust and develop relationships. But imagine coming in as the leader of a team where, by organization, everybody is looking at you, wondering who you are, what you're about, and expecting that level of guidance.

Not only are you learning your new job and learning what issues need tackling, but you're also assessing the people on your team and trying to figure out their competencies. Just one of those things is enough to do. Trying to juggle all of them is a challenge.

I remember one of the first staff meetings I held, where everybody came in and expected me to tell them what to do. They explained a situation and asked me what they should do. I said, "Well, what do you think you should do?" They were like deer in the headlights because they weren't used to being allowed to think for themselves.

In that first year or two, I think I often came across as though I didn't know what I was doing because I would ask people what they thought they should do instead of just telling them. But I was really trying to get them to be more comfortable thinking for themselves.

Leadership Lessons . . .

If the people on your team are always looking for you to tell them what to do and which way to go, then you've limited yourself to only being as good as the person who is leading because you always have to look to that person for guidance.

When you have someone who just doesn't mix with the rest of the team, or who is being disruptive, you need to have the courage to move them out of that team, or even out of the organization. If you don't, it will only create more conflict within your team, or in some cases, within your whole organization.

You don't always have to be the smartest person in the room. Letting go of that and making space for others to step up will help the development of your leaders and their teams.

IDENTIFYING THE UNDERLYING ROOT OF CONFLICT

We often think of conflict management in terms of managing people—egos, in some cases; different personality types and how people interact with each other—or in terms of managing emotions because everybody is human and every now and then people bring their emotions into the team or a meeting.

But I believe that on an organizational level, at the heart of every conflict you'll find resources. The majority of organizations have limited resources. At this level, you don't have all the resources you'd like to solve the issues you're facing. Resources can be people, money, or time, and they span an entire organization.

At an executive level, a team is operating at its healthiest when people are stepping outside of their departmental needs and looking at the overall requirements of the organization and the effect that its resources have on customers or clients. This is when you can start to have authentic and healthy conversations about resources.

For example, at PRECorp in the months following the Covid-19 pandemic our sales were declining because of some downturns in the energy industry. Our expenses were naturally going up, and we couldn't automatically increase the price of our product to make up for falling sales volumes and rising expenses. When this happens, people and teams start to compete for resources within the organization. A good leader should be aware of this kind of conflict.

If you don't recognize that source of conflict, and bring people together to remind them of the mission and vision of your organization, even the best people will start to lose sight of that. The fabric of your team starts to get damaged, and that can manifest itself as bickering between departments or teams. But the actual underlying cause of these conflicts is resources.

This is an issue we were facing at PRECorp as I wrote the first version of this book. We had been cutting costs and carrying out cost containment for a long time and we had done a pretty good job of reducing most extraneous expenses, but that meant we had reached the stage where trimming more areas would be really painful.

When you're in a situation like that, it's important to remind the team of the bigger picture. You should return to the larger purpose behind your organization, because if your teams aren't aware of or don't recall that larger purpose, organization and team cohesiveness start to get really tough when teams are competing for resources.

As I said, most people won't recognize that the conflicts stem from this competition for resources. But, as a leader, being aware of the underlying reason for conflict within a team, or between teams, is one of the most important elements to help you successfully manage conflict. You need to dig deeper and look beyond what's obvious to find the root cause of the conflict; and resource conflicts are one of the biggest underlying issues, in my experience.

How to Manage Resource Conflicts

At PRECorp, we were communicating the bigger issues that we faced with everyone in the organization. We were open about our declining sales and our ongoing efforts to reduce expenses. We were also leveraging accelerating technologies to reduce our costs and digitizing processes as much as possible. As the leader of that organization, I had to communicate the landscape that we were in to all of our employees.

As in most businesses, the executive team included the people who needed to take a deep dive into the gory details of what we were doing to survive in that landscape. The executive staff needed to be aware of the landscape they were working in and what the major conflicts were. This awareness helped prevent the resource allocation issues from manifesting as bickering between departments or teams, or even within the executive team itself.

The executive team's job was to create a plan to deal with these underlying sources of conflict and to find a clear path through. There will definitely be trade-offs in this kind of situation. Some departments or functions within departments might change or completely be eliminated. Sacrifices have to be made, but the trick to doing this successfully and constructively is for the executive staff to have a solid understanding of the conflict that they're trying to solve.

At this stage, it evolves into a negotiation within the executive team to determine how to use the resources your organization has to meet its purpose as closely as you can, without your members suffering too much.

Once you've created a plan that the executive team signs off on, the objective then becomes how you can deliver that to the team and facilitate the results of your decision making.

This is where real leadership comes in. It can be so easy for the person who's offering up resources from their part of the company to help a different area altogether to assume a victim mentality or blame others within the business if they are losing resources.

True Leaders Worth Following make sure that everyone is reminded of the organization's overall purpose, so once a decision like this is made, the executive team is communicating it to their teams, and so on. This helps teams who are making sacrifices understand that it's for the greater good, and shows them that they're contributing to the overall mission of the business.

This approach also means that teams who benefit from the resources taken from elsewhere understand that these resources come with a sacrifice. Hopefully, what happens is that these teams appreciate what's been done and, therefore, are more diligent with the resources they've been given and are more focused on delivering the expected return for the organization.

Reframing changes and resource allocation in this way means that people across your organization are more likely to support them. They see those resources as a gift and, therefore, try to do well with that gift. I believe this is the kind of leadership that you get out of a really high-functioning team that's able to dip below the apparent conflicts to get to the heart of their causes, which are often resource related.

Being able to come up with a plan that keeps the company's purpose as the ultimate objective is the next step. From here, it's about delivering those results in such a way that all of your team members feel empowered by the direction that the company is going and the changes that are being made, rather than feeling victimized.

MIKE'S LEADERSHIP LESSON: BUSINESS RESOURCES

As I said earlier, at PRECorp we were more resource-constrained in 2020–21 than we ever had been. Covid-19 played a big part in that; but in our case, it also had to do with how the energy industry was changing at that time.

I explained the concept that I've just unpacked with my executive team. I held a meeting and I told them that I wanted to talk about the changes emerging in the energy industry that we would be facing. I said that I knew things had been getting tighter, we had been cutting expenses to become more efficient, and we were continually looking at ways to do more with fewer resources. I also told them that we were reaching the point where we'd be cutting to the bone in some areas.

"I'm concerned that, as a result, we're going to see conflict come up that nobody's prepared to deal with," I said. Then I went on to explain this concept of competition for resources between business departments, and I pointed out that, within the world in general, competition for resources underlies many conflicts.

"What's going to happen is that all the areas of conflict that we've had before, that we think we've resolved, are going to rear their ugly heads again, and it's going to feel as though that's the conflict. But in actual fact, we have this resource conflict underpinning them," I said.

After this conversation with my team, I shared this narrative with the entire company, although I framed it slightly differently and said that we may be experiencing more conflict in the immediate future, and the reason for this conflict was potentially deeper than we realized. I asked everyone to think about that, and when they experienced any conflict, to remember their mission and to look at the bigger picture.

Fast forward a few days, I was having one-on-one meetings with members of my executive team. People were coming to me very concerned, and the conversations started with, "Were you talking about me? In that conversation were you trying to send me a message? Were you trying to tell me that I need to be a team player? Did somebody tell you that I wasn't a team player? Because here are all the reasons why I am a team player . . ."

They each reeled off a huge list of things that they were feeling anxious about in relation to everybody else. They all took this conversation very personally, as though I had been talking about them doing something that wasn't right.

In response I said, "This wasn't something that I was telling the team that we're doing. My whole purpose was to equip you to understand that we may be feeling more anxiety about certain things (that feel like normal things to feel anxiety about) but that, in actual fact, are a sign of an underlying issue. Maybe you're feeling some anxiety, like I was talking about . . ."

At this point, the conversation became totally different. "So you weren't talking about me?" "No." "You were talking about how I might be feeling anxiety and concern that I maybe haven't felt recently?" "Yes."

This realization was followed by a long, uncomfortable silence where I could see each person self-reflect and think, "Oh man, I'm *feeling* things."

Leadership Lessons . . .

Conflict in business or work is like any emotional conflict that we encounter or any problem that we fear. If you can name it, you can fix it.

When you're leading a team and you're managing conflict, it's important to help people name what they're feeling. You don't even have to get it exactly right, but if you can name it in a way that allows people to look at it, talk about it, feel it, and deal with it, you can find a resolution.

This then moves into the process of negotiation, where you talk about the various trade-offs that may resolve the conflict. In a proper conflict resolution, everybody moves a little toward a compromise. Nobody gets exactly what they want; there is always give and take. But it's the ability to name the issue and step back from it that allows you to stop feeling it and start talking about it. This will lead you to the point of negotiating, brainstorming, and problem solving to figure out what you can do to move forward.

It's necessary as the leader to make sure you're guiding your team through this. To do that, you have to step outside of yourself and see it from an observer's perspective. You can't be in there with them, but you're there to guide people as they reflect on their emotions, experience the conflict, and finally get ready to negotiate and resolve it.

As a leader you need to see conflicts from all perspectives to enable you to help everyone navigate those in a healthy and constructive way.

KEEP YOUR EYE ON THE PURPOSE

Most companies will have a stated purpose or mission, and some teams may also have a stated purpose. If you're the leader of a team, or the leader of many teams, it's your job to know yourself and communicate what that purpose is with your people.

You have to keep your eye on the purpose. It can help if you can connect that team or organizational purpose to a worthwhile cause that is bigger than the self, because that helps people to step out of themselves and focus on that broader purpose.

Hopefully, you, or the leaders before you, have already established what that bigger purpose is. As you resolve conflict, it's important to keep everybody focused on that bigger purpose, and on the reason for them being there and for giving their time and energy to that purpose.

SELF-AWARENESS IS KEY FOR ENCOURAGING SELF-AWARENESS IN OTHERS

If you want to move yourself further along the path towards becoming A Leader Worth Following, and in doing so, shift from being a good leader to being a great leader, you have to be aware of what's going on inside yourself.

You have to follow your feelings, which can be a scary thought, especially if you're an engineer like me. I would say I spent two-thirds of my career thinking that feelings were an impediment. I believed that if you felt a certain way about something you had to block those feelings in order to make decisions. I was lucky enough to get through those first two-thirds of my career without doing too much damage to myself or the others around me despite having this belief.

This concept of having self-awareness ties back into the continuum we're talking about in this book, of moving from self-leadership, to leading others, to leading organizations. As I said in the first part of the book, the way you lead yourself is to pay attention to what's going on inside you by becoming aware of your feelings and emotions and thinking about them.

Going back to the example I gave in my leadership lesson, where my managers were coming to me with all of this anxiety—I remember one manager in particular who was passionately justifying why he was a team player and part of me wanted to jump in and engage with him there.

But because of my ability to take a step back and view the situation from an outside perspective, I was able to think about what I was feeling and why I was feeling that way. In my experience, often when you're talking to somebody and you begin to feel anxious or angry, or you feel emotional energy building up, there's a good chance that it's *their* emotional energy coming at you.

At this point, you have two choices: you can enter the game and feed that back to them, in which case it often escalates, or you can recognize the emotion and the fact that it's developed during this conversation. This allows you to see that it's the other person who's feeling anxious, and that enables you to step back and make a conscious decision about how to move the conversation forward rather than allowing it to be hijacked by that emotional energy.

Self-leadership is deciding to take that different tack and, as a leader, you model that for the people around you. When you do that for yourself, you're then able to help others do that also.

Sometimes you might decide that you need to engage emotionally with someone, rather than take the calm approach. If you do that, you have to make sure you're intentionally engaging emotionally and not being reactive, though. The less you can react and the more you can do things with intention, the better.

If you're not paying attention to that energy, that's when you can get into trouble, because it becomes a back-and-forth thing and the energy escalates. Your aim should be to de-escalate that energy and bring it down to a manageable level because when emotions get high, we lose our ability to think rationally.

COPING WITH AN UNEVEN POWER DIFFERENTIAL

There may be situations where you're on the wrong side of an uneven power differential, or when you're facing a group of people who are ramped up with this energy. My advice in this situation is not to panic and to let it wash over you instead.

It's a lot like being in the ocean with waves crashing over you. You know what's coming, you brace for it, and the waves crash around you. But all of a sudden, a really big wave comes with a lot of energy and you fight it as it crashes over you. The next thing you know, you're being pushed against the sand, there's a tumble of white water, you're getting rolled with the current, and you feel lost, scared, and maybe even for a moment, as though your world is coming to an end. As the wave passes through, you finally break the surface, gasping for breath.

The other option in this scenario is not to fight the big wave that comes crashing down around you, but to flow with it and glide with it. As the wave passes through, it takes you with it, but you put your feet down and stand up, realizing that you're only in knee-deep water.

When you're in a meeting or interacting with someone where there's this uneven power differential, think about it as that wave that's going to crash over you. You can't stop it and you can't change it. If you fight it, it will take control and push you under, but if you flow with it and go with the energy of that wave, you'll end up in shallower water where you can stand and be in a much better position where you're ready to connect more rationally.

Staying calm and not panicking allows you to connect rationally with that group or that person, even if you have to wait for a few more waves to hit you before you find the right moment to connect in that way.

PART 3

MANAGING AND LEADING/ ORGANIZATION FOCUS

Managing and leading an organization is the next step on your leadership journey once you're effectively managing teams, just as effectively managing a team was the natural follow up to being able to lead yourself. This is simply the next stage in the continuum of your growth as a leader, which all started with self-management.

Every step along the way, you're dealing with increased complexity, and leading an organization is where your ability to live, work, and deal with complexity becomes very important.

Complexity in this sense, especially as you're dealing with people, is about how comfortable you are dealing with uncertainty and how easily you can take a step back to look at multiple, possibly conflicting, ideas with a view to finding a path forward that is the best choice for the organization. Leading an organization is essentially managing several different teams, and your role is to engage all of these teams to move toward the organization's goals.

The more effective you are as a leader at creating a vision that everybody understands and can buy into, the more successful you'll be at engaging teams and influencing them to accomplish what needs to be done. This is also a sign that you're making progress on your journey to becoming A Leader Worth Following.

Underpinning your ability to manage multiple teams, manage an organization, and move the people within that organization towards a common goal, you should understand what organizations are and how they work.

As someone who is leading an organization, you should be able to think and look ahead, at least as far as anyone within your teams, and, ideally, farther than them.

Think of it in terms of a car's headlights. As the leader, your view is like the headlights on a car at night. You need to cast that view farther ahead than anyone else who works in the organization. If you can't do that, then you're likely to encounter conflict.

Vision is this ability to think in complex terms, operate in areas of the unknown, and consider a whole range of factors to make assumptions that, more often than not, are correct. As you begin to lead organizations, being aware of what vision looks like and where your vision lines up with the teams you're leading is very important. Where your vision doesn't match or exceed the teams you're leading, you'll struggle to find success.

Your ability to engage and leverage teams depends on you having that overarching vision and being able to imagine further into the future than anyone else.

As you move along the leadership continuum, the more important it is to be self-aware. Understanding what's driving you and why you're making certain decisions is extremely crucial as you lead other people and lead an organization.

A large part of leadership involves making decisions. Some decisions you can make quickly, but others will be slow. When you first start leading organizations, you will most likely have a rigorous process for making decisions and spend a lot of time thinking about them. You'll get into the consequences of those decisions, not only in terms of how they affect your immediate team, but also the teams they lead and the people within those teams.

As you gain experience, decision making becomes easier. Humans are best at recognizing patterns and the more decisions you make, the more likely you are to come across patterns that you've seen before, which will eventually mean you may not need to carry out that detailed level of analysis every time.

Experienced leaders successful at leading teams and organizations have developed a vast portfolio of pattern recognition to help them know what to do. But even when you have this experience, there are three things you should always bear in mind as you're making decisions. I call them the "No-Os of Leadership," and I'll share more about them in Part 4 of this book.

We're going to start Part 3, however, by looking more closely at engaging teams across an organization and guiding your teams toward the best outcomes.

>>>>>>>>>>>>>>>>>>>>>>>>>>>>>>>>>>>>>

CHAPTER 9

ENGAGING TEAMS

"Engaged employees translate to engaged teams and that translates to an effective organization."

Engaging teams in this context centers around how you develop and unify multiple teams to work toward a common goal. As someone who is leading multiple teams, your aim is to figure out how to get them to work together in the most effective way for your organization.

To scale this up to an organizational level, you need a solid understanding of teamwork. You need to plan and organize around developing teamwork and engaging your teams; and in doing so, you'll ultimately be pursuing excellence through the efforts that your teams are making, as well as delivering on the overall mission or purpose of the organization.

DEVELOPING TEAMWORK

Developing teamwork is important for anyone who is good at managing and leading, and who is focused on the needs of the overall organization. But developing teamwork is actually very counterintuitive, and the mistake you could make is thinking that you're going to be the one who is developing teamwork, getting in there, moving pieces around, and pulling levers; and that couldn't be further from the truth.

People who are able to lead organizations don't develop teamwork by telling everybody what to do. They develop teamwork by creating systems and ways of thinking about problem solving and how people relate to each other. As a leader at this organizational level, you have to create a culture that allows people to work independently without your day-to-day input.

By the time you're leading an organization, you've followed and understood the ideas and concepts in the first two parts of this book. At this point, you have team leaders who are very competent and self-aware, and who are doing a good job with their teams. They're on the road to becoming Leaders Worth Following. Your job, as the leader of the organization, is to bring all of that together and stand back. That's the end game. If you do such a good job of developing your people and your teams that this is the result, you bounce between feeling really proud that they can function without you and really scared that they can function without you. It's a double-edged sword.

If you look at an organization that's highly successful, functioning well, and highly adaptive, and peel back the layers, you get down to the people within that organization. What you find when you reach the people is that they each have a clear understanding of the organization's overall vision, as well as their role in it and contribution toward it.

What I've discovered is that what makes an organization successful is all the individuals within the organization know how they can contribute personally to its success. That's the first step in developing teamwork: everyone understands what the big-picture goal is and how they contribute to that.

❙ *"Leaders Worth Following are willing to teach."*

Once you have that individual level of understanding, you bring them together in teams and help them understand how they contribute to their team, as well as how their team interacts with other teams to accomplish that vision. This is why having a clear, compelling vision is so important. Again, this comes back to the concept of having a noble cause involved, which can help people engage individually, which in turn brings teams together.

The other thing that's very important in developing teamwork is that the culture of your company invites feedback from your employees and teams. I'm not just talking about asking for feedback, but also making sure that you do something with that feedback.

Companies that are highly successful have a deliberate and dependable process for gathering feedback from their entire team and then using that feedback to eliminate friction within the organization to make the organization a better place for everybody to work.

The feedback system you introduce needs to make people feel comfortable expressing their opinions, and the results of the feedback need to be open and transparent.

A company that collects employee feedback but doesn't share it or doesn't do anything with it isn't going to be successful. You should be showing your employees, year after year, what feedback you received, what you did with it, and how acting on it has contributed to the overall success of the company. Taking action on that feedback is important.

Doing that regularly and consistently will help create a sense of teamwork, not only in the sense that everybody is on the same team from the bigger perspective, but also that there's a sense of alignment among people on separate teams and the understanding that their thoughts and opinions do make a difference to the organization. This creates buy-in and engaged employees. Engaged employees translate to engaged teams and that translates to an effective organization.

The final area to focus on in terms of developing teamwork is demonstrating a commitment to your employees by providing training and development for people. Remember, this is one of the key elements of becoming A Leader Worth Following—being willing to teach. One of the strongest ways to develop teamwork, and to develop people in the process, is by providing opportunities for people to work cross-functionally.

Teamwork is everybody on a team working together in the same direction, but you can scale that across an organization by focusing on this concept of cross-functional working and training.

When different teams and different people from across the organization have an opportunity to work together, it creates a real sense of camaraderie. Similarly, giving people the chance to be part of a cross-functional training and development program accelerates that feeling of teamwork across a company and the silos within that company are reduced.

At this stage, people relate not only to others within their team, but also cross-functionally within the organization; and this is when an organization itself feels like a team rather than a disparate bunch of teams who are working loosely together.

Having a compelling vision with each individual understanding their role in accomplishing that vision; giving individuals the opportunity to provide feedback and knowing that their opinions matter; and providing cross-functional developmental opportunities are the best ways to develop teamwork in the sense that your entire organization is a team.

ALIGNING EXTERNAL TEAMS WITH YOUR COMPANY VISION

This idea of everyone being aligned with your overall company vision extends to any external contractors, partners, or teams that you might be working with. When you're leading at an organizational level and you form partnerships or relationships with key vendors or contributors outside your organization, they need to understand your company's culture. There should be at least some alignment in culture, and if your culture doesn't align with that of a vendor or contractor, you're inviting friction into your organization.

As you look to develop relationships outside of your organization to help you accomplish your vision, it helps for you to share your vision so they understand what you're about and why it is that you do what you do. You don't need to be perfectly aligned, but those external vendors, entities, and partners need to understand their roles and how they fit into your culture in order for you to work well together.

PLANNING AND ORGANIZING

Imagine that your organization is an Olympic athlete who is constantly training and constantly improving. You start to make minor shifts to the way you hold your body, or maybe move your hand, in order to improve your performance.

The organizational version of this is that everyone brings their own set of skills, passions, strengths, and weaknesses to the organization. Many times, a person's position may not actually play to what they're really passionate about or particularly good at. This is where you, as the leader, have to be planning and organizing to make sure that you have the right people in the right seats on the bus.

For example, an issue often encountered within companies is an employee performing a particular job that they're not especially good at or where they're struggling with certain aspects of a job. As a leader we may be tempted to think, "That person isn't cutting it; we need to get somebody else to do that job."

However, we need to step back from that approach and instead take the time to really understand that person. Maybe that employee's skill set isn't quite right for where that position is currently or where it's evolved to, but perhaps their skill set is suited better for another job. Think about whether there are other places in your organization where that person's contribution can be fully felt and where you can harness their passion.

An important element of planning and organizing your company is having talent move intentionally around your organization. Consider the costs of hiring someone new and what you have to invest in them to not only train them in their tasks, but also in helping them to understand how they align with the company's vision. You don't want to lose good employees because they feel a job has run its course or it's not meeting their passion.

In fact, encouraging people to understand their alignment to the company vision can even help them to self-explore and determine whether their skills and talents are contributing to the company. As a leader you want to enable those frank conversations, not only from a performance perspective, but also from the perspective of personal development.

You ideally want to have those conversations way before you have performance issues, and it's much easier to approach people about this internal movement when you understand what they're passionate about and where their strengths lie.

Plan for the development and personal growth of your people and align that with the growth of the organization. Intentionally moving talent around your organization ensures that everybody is contributing their best self to the broader mission.

This is important for leaders to recognize—and it's particularly important for the person who's running an organization to recognize—because it makes much more sense to lose people to other positions within your organization than to lose them to outside companies.

In addition, when people see opportunities for growth within the organization and understand how they fit in, it gives them even more reasons to develop teamwork and commitment to the company.

MENTORSHIP: DEVELOPING TALENT AND PURSUING EXCELLENCE

Over the years I spent learning from Ken Blanchard, he taught me we are the average of the eight people that we interact with and value the most, not only at work but in many areas of our lives. When looking for ways to help further develop the talent in your team to enable others to pursue excellence, mentoring is an obvious place to start.

You can have informal and formal mentors in your life, but what I'm talking about here is having a formal mentorship relationship. This means you're describing it as such and dedicating time to building that relationship. The words you use in relation to being a mentor, or a mentee, are important because words create intention and intention creates outcome. I believe you need to have that intention to get the most out of mentorship in a leadership context. We can all benefit from having mentors at any stage in our career, and we will also get positives from being a mentor for others.

If you are looking for a mentor to further your leadership journey, it's important to find someone who has the qualities and values that you are trying to seek. You're looking for someone whose character and values will rub off on you and make you better for the time you spend with them.

Depending on why you're looking for a mentor, you may also be seeking someone with a specific skill that you want to develop further, or someone with expertise or insight in an area that you are working on personally. The act of seeking out a mentor shows your commitment to your leadership journey and that you are seeking to improve yourself.

MIKE'S LEADERSHIP LESSON: DO YOU DO CHARITY WORK?

At the time of 9/11, I'd been CEO at PRECorp for a little over a year. When 9/11 happened, I remember feeling a call to leadership and service that manifested as "I've got to do better and up my game." Understandably, after 9/11 there was a lot of fear in the country. At PRECorp, we decided to run an initiative called our "Celebration of Community Champions."

Super Bowl champions Kevin Holloway and William Perry got involved. We did a bus tour across our service territory, and we created a lot of positive energy by celebrating volunteers and their communities. This initiative resulted in an invitation to speak at an annual meeting of the National Electrical Cooperative Association. That's where I met Kevin Freiberg.

Kevin was a panel moderator at that meeting and, after his presentation, I did something bold. I approached him and asked, "Do you do any charity work?" He looked at me kind of funny and said, "What do you mean?" I replied, "Well, I work for a not-for-profit, as a CEO. We don't have a lot of money and I'm sure I can't afford you but if you do any charity work I sure would appreciate your help." He laughed, told me to give him a call, and follow up with him.

That conversation resulted in Kevin coaching me, helping me with strategic planning at PRECorp, and has led to a really interesting relationship that I value to this day (you might have noticed that Kevin wrote the foreword to this book).

Leadership Lessons . . .

I was at the beginning of my journey as a cooperative CEO and I recognized I could benefit from support from someone with more experience. That awareness was what made me see how Kevin could support me as I developed and grew into my leadership role.

The important thing is that I didn't shrink away and hide from what I noticed—I faced reality and owned my weaknesses. I found the courage to ask Kevin for his help. The worst that could have happened was that he said no, but by having the courage to approach him, I found an understanding and supportive mentor who has been part of my leadership journey for many years.

Understanding where you need guidance will help you identify the right people to mentor you at different stages in your leadership journey, and to do that you need self-awareness. The journey towards becoming A Leader Worth Following is long, and sometimes it's nice to have some company on the road, especially if that person has traveled this road before.

As a leader within an organization, you may have an opportunity to mentor some of the people within your teams. This is part of giving back as a leader and being willing to teach, because we all have a unique set of skills and abilities that make us special. Having the ability to share those with others puts you in a position to be a mentor.

When you become a mentor, part of your role is to hold up a mirror for your mentee to help them more clearly see their strengths, areas to improve, and opportunities for growth. As a mentor, you also have to understand how best to hold that mirror up for different people so that you can provide each individual with feedback in a way that works for them.

Building rapport and trust is an important part of the mentor–mentee relationship. You have to be able to sit with your mentee without judgment and accept them where they are. You'll give them feedback, but you'll do it in a meaningful, tactful, and caring way. When you have this rapport and trust, both of you will take positives from your relationship.

Giving the people within your teams the opportunity to find and work with mentors in your organization is incredibly powerful and encourages everyone to pursue excellence in their own way. For me, being both a mentee and a mentor is an opportunity to get better at what I do. A large part of becoming A Leader Worth Following is having self-awareness, as I've explained already; and embracing mentorship, whether you take the role of student or teacher, is an opportunity to get better at what you do and to grow as a person.

WHY BECOME A MENTOR AND HOW TO DO IT

Many of us are aware of the benefits of being a mentee and having a mentor, but there is a great deal to gain from becoming a mentor for others who are at a different stage of their leadership journey. The further along your journey you get, the more opportunities you will have to give back in this way.

Mentorship is all about building relationships, learning from each other, sharing, teaching, and experiencing, all of which means you will benefit whichever side of the relationship you're on. As you now know, this also supports you as you become A Leader Worth Following.

Around the time I was writing the first edition of this book, a young man was appointed CEO at another cooperative, and he had moved into that role from one in senior management. Because I remembered what it felt like when I first took the reins of leadership like that, how frightening it was at times, and how I definitely made some missteps, I phoned this guy and said, "Hey, I know this is all new, and I know what it feels like to be starting out on this journey. I think you're going to be great at it, but if there's anything I can do to help, or you think me sharing my experiences could help you get better faster, then I'd be more than willing to do that." We spoke every two weeks after I made this call until I retired from my position at PRECorp.

I put myself out there and volunteered to be his mentor, not because I felt that he had any specific weaknesses, but because I've been on that journey and I know how valuable that support can be. I also made a commitment to him and to myself that I would be available for those calls every two weeks. It's important to make that time commitment and to honor it, both for your mentee and for yourself.

However, these calls with this new CEO weren't only beneficial for him; they helped me too. I learned from him, and our conversations reminded me of things that are still good to know, even after all these years. Like I said in Chapter 1, when you teach something, you relearn it all over again.

If you want to volunteer to be someone's mentor, approach the conversation with thought and empathy. If there's someone who seems to be struggling, or who you feel you could help, make yourself available to help them without taking away their sense of power or, as it's often called, their sense of agency.

My advice, if you see someone struggling, is to first ask them for permission to give them feedback. The conversation might go a little something like this: "Hey, I've been watching you and I think you do a great job, but I noticed this one thing and I wondered if you'd be open to some feedback on this?" More often than not, that person will say "yes," and if they don't, then you know that they aren't open to this kind of relationship at this time.

The first few times you approach someone to offer support in this way, it might feel strange. You might question yourself and what makes you feel you're an expert in this area, but please, trust in your intentions being good and work through those feelings. We all have the voice of "I'm not . . ." inside of us. It tells us things like, "I'm not good enough; I'm not smart enough; I'm not strong enough. . . ." You get the idea. There can be times in our lives when that voice seems to be yelling at us. However, what we always have to do, both in our capacity as leaders and in our lives in general, is be aware of that voice and find a way to shut it down. It's common for this voice of "I'm not . . ." to pop up when you're offering to teach someone something, but always remember that you have a set of unique skills and strengths, the combination of which isn't like anyone else's.

If you find this voice of "I'm not . . ." starting to shout when you either offer to mentor someone or are asked to support someone in this way, take a moment to remind yourself that you are good at what you do, you do have talent, you do have individuality, and you can contribute in many different ways.

Remember, too, that this relationship isn't only about you sharing your knowledge and experiences with someone else. It's an opportunity for you to learn, as well as to teach. You, and the person you are supporting, are both pursuing excellence.

There is a very powerful concept called "beginner's mind," which means that in some cases people who are new to something might approach it in a different way than someone who has been doing the activity for a long time. They don't have preconceptions about how something should be done, and no one has told them that something can't be done. When you share how you would approach a particular task or situation, be humble and allow the person you are talking to the space to build on your approach. The best way to get the most out of the mentor–mentee relationship is to view it as a learning experience for yourself, as well as an opportunity to help somebody else.

YOU ARE THE ONLY PERSON THAT YOU HAVE THE POWER TO CHANGE

It's very powerful to remember that you are the only person that you have the power to change. Leaders Worth Following change themselves first and lead by example. The truth is, you can't change anybody else, and trying to do so is often frustrating. When you go into a relationship as a mentor, go into it with humility, and remember that you are there to support the other person, not to "fix" them.

I can tell you, from my years of experience, that trying to "fix" people doesn't work. I have certainly made the mistake of trying, but this never achieves the outcome I'm looking for. What I have learned is that I can support people and I can help them see a possible future, but they have to build that future for themselves. When you're striving to become A Leader Worth Following, you're holding space for that person and being supportive, rather than giving them instructions on what to do.

If someone comes to you with problems or challenges that they want to discuss, resist the urge to tell them what you would do and instead ask them, "What do you think you might want to do about that?" Give them a safe space where they can talk about their thoughts and find their own answers. It can be challenging, but you have to allow people to figure things out for themselves. People can fix and grow themselves, but this isn't a process that can be forced or one that you have the power to control.

IDENTIFYING YOUR PASSION

If you are new to being a mentor and are unsure of where to begin, my advice is to think about what you're passionate about—both in and out of the workplace. What do you really enjoy doing? Do you lose track of time when you're working on a particular project, and suddenly realize that two hours have gone by in what feels like a flash? The answers to both of those questions are good indicators of things that come naturally to you and that are your strengths.

When you're trying to identify what aspect of your work you're most passionate about, ask yourself that question about losing track of time. When you feel like this, you have entered a flow state, which, without going into too much of the science behind it, means that all the parts of your brain are fully engaged in working on that task or project. Identifying what causes you to enter a flow state is a good starting point for recognizing the skills and areas you might be able to offer others to help them grow and learn.

OPEN COMMUNICATION ENHANCES TEAMWORK

Developing mentor–mentee relationships encourages open and honest communication, which is essential for fostering an environment that encourages strong teamwork. However, this is just one way in which to create open communication in a business.

There's no doubt that teamwork is enhanced in a culture where there's open communication. It's important for people to have a line of sight from who they are and what they do to the ultimate vision and purpose of the company. That's critical to get engagement.

It follows that, if you want people to be engaged in the organization to that level and have that sense of teamwork, you need to communicate. Communication is the lubrication for that engagement, and it's an essential piece of the puzzle because it feeds engagement and it feeds people.

> *"Leading with empathy will help you to empower, and if you can empower others they will, in turn, embrace your leadership."*

As more employees move to working remotely, your communication has to increase. Communication isn't just talking *at* people; it's talking *with* people, and it's everybody's job. How leaders model communication, especially when people are under stress, is critical to maintaining the sense of team and the sense of togetherness when people are working remotely.

If supervisors understand this, then they're going to be communicating more with their people. If you're leading an organization, you have to communicate with people in new and different ways. At PRECorp, for instance, we became much more comfortable with video communications.

In 2020, I started doing a quick update to the whole team every two weeks. This was an all-company online Zoom meeting where I communicated content and challenges to the team in a way that they had never seen before. I gave them an insight into the big picture, as well as some of the day-to-day challenges that we were facing as a company, and that I was facing as a CEO. I think people felt more informed and committed as a result.

This bi-monthly dialogue created a sense of teamwork and unity. When you think about it, people everywhere want to have a sense of belonging, and when they have that it creates personal resilience. Being honest and communicating regularly with everyone in my company while I was CEO is an example of teamwork. We all like to belong to a team because it creates that sense of belonging that we, as humans, crave. That sense of belonging also feeds teamwork.

By being honest, authentic, and showing some vulnerability in my communications with my team, particularly around the challenges we were facing, I was able to reassure them that we were all in it together and that, in turn, fostered that sense of belonging.

People are more accepting of video communications than they were before the pandemic, and I think this is a great opportunity for leaders to maintain a closer relationship with their teams. I used to have an annual meeting where we'd pull everyone in the company together physically and I'd tell them what was going on and discussed challenges the company was experiencing. If you ask people now if they'd like me to go back to doing an annual meeting with all the pomp and ceremony, or to continue with the twice-weekly, 20-minute Zoom meetings, I think they'd much rather have the shorter, more frequent communications.

MIKE'S LEADERSHIP LESSON: OPEN-DOOR POLICY

As CEO, I always had an open-door policy where anyone could come and see me at any time and talk to me about anything.

Early on, many employees would take advantage of my open-door policy. They'd come and talk to me about issues, and I would feel like these were issues I had to fix. I would then try to reach down the organization to fix them, but I learned pretty quickly that wasn't the way to do it, because it didn't work well for anyone.

Of course, there might be instances where there's harassment going on or policy violations you have to get involved with because you have a duty of care as a leader. But for the most part, I took this feedback as a datapoint and used that time to connect with the people in the organization and get a sense of where things were.

I thanked people for their information, I let them feel valued for taking the time to speak to me and, in doing that, people felt valued and heard. Sometimes there were opportunities for me to make a suggestion or ask a question related to what the person talked to me about in a one-on-one, but I didn't directly intervene.

With the Covid-19 pandemic things obviously changed, and I tried to take my open-door policy to the next level. That meant I tried to have one-on-one Zoom meetings with all my team members. My aim was to have spoken to each of my employees, one-on-one, by the end of 2020; and I did manage to speak to the majority of them on this level. I was having two or three calls each day. Sometimes these calls lasted five minutes, sometimes 25 minutes.

My first questions in these calls were, "How are you doing? How's it going for you? How is your family?" People have different family situations, with some people's families near and others far away. Some of them had pretty tough things happen in their families during this year, and I felt that it was my duty as CEO to check in with them to get a sense of how my team members and, ultimately the organization, were doing.

Leadership Lessons . . .

It's important if you're adopting an open-door policy as a CEO that you manage this in the right way. In some organizations, this could be concerning for other managers who worry about their teams having a direct pipeline to the CEO.

I believe it's valuable for people leading teams, including CEOs, to be open to hearing what other people have to say. That being said, that doesn't mean that if you hear something you have to fix it or act on it.

If you develop the trust of your leadership team and your supervisors, they will know that the open-door policy you have as a CEO is valuable, and the outcomes from what you hear from people are informative, not reactive. People shouldn't feel like there has been a violation of the chain of command. You don't want your managers to feel threatened by you, as the CEO, connecting to your employees at that one-on-one level.

Having teams that are healthy enough, and having the ability as CEO to dive in and connect with your employees to have that dialogue in an environment where no one thinks twice about it is a pretty great goal and a worthy outcome.

As a leader, this allowed me to gather data points on how the organization was doing, and it was a great opportunity to put my finger on the pulse of the organization and to know how my people were doing. Making that personal connection is pretty powerful stuff, and it's important to think about how, as leaders, we can continue to influence that in the future.

Meeting people where they are and putting yourself in their shoes is what will help you, as a leader, build those personal connections. It's all about having empathy and a great heart.

CHAPTER 10

LEVERAGING TEAMS

"When you empower your people, you will have even greater success and get even more satisfaction from your employees, while at the same time taking yourself to a different level."

As you move into managing and leading at an organizational level, you're not just leading one team any more, you're leading several teams and trying to keep everyone moving in the same direction to accomplish the goals within your organization.

One of the most important talents for leaders to have at this level is the ability to step back, watch those different teams, and see how they work. In terms of influencing your teams to accomplish those goals, I've found cross-functional teams are particularly important.

In any organization, nothing gets done in a vacuum. There are lots of opportunities, if you want to take them, to increase collaboration by creating cross-functional teams that can bring people from across your company together to get things done. However, accomplishing goals and completing tasks is far from the only benefit to establishing cross-functional teams.

USING CROSS-FUNCTIONAL TEAMS TO DEVELOP PEOPLE

A bigger reason why we created cross-functional teams at PRECorp was to develop people, give them different experiences, and expose them to different people in the organization, which then builds teamwork.

This involves looking beyond the input and output of a particular team. As a leader, you're examining the process of how you put teams together, who you put on those teams, and what breadth of cross-functional experience you need. In considering these elements, you create opportunities for people to develop within those teams.

When you're creating these teams, you'll notice that some will really click and do well, while others might struggle. Part of your job, when it comes to creating teams, is to be able to look at those that are struggling and diagnose where the issues might be. It's not your job to jump in and fix things, though. Once you're at this level of leadership you'll be supporting the leaders of those teams, and the teams themselves, to work through any issues or challenges they encounter.

MIKE'S LEADERSHIP LESSON: JENNY

Jenny was a hard-working employee whose job dedication caught my attention. I noticed that she had a can-do attitude, she wanted to get the job done, she took pride in her work, and she wanted to make a difference. If she told you that she was going to do something and made it a commitment, she wouldn't let you down.

Jenny was the type of person who wasn't afraid to try something new, she wasn't afraid of change, and she was always willing to go the extra mile. She had an incredible ability to internalize a commitment to every member of the team for the duration of a project. If you wanted a team to work well, she was someone you would put on that team, but what was more important was that other people were excited to work with her.

When other people heard that Jenny was on a team, they became excited about the possibility of being on that team too. They wanted to be part of it, feel her energy, and they knew she was a good team member and enjoyed working with her.

My thought was that the more people we could expose to her, the better they were going to get, but also the better she was going to get.

Leadership Lessons . . .

Diagnosing teams isn't only about getting them to accomplish certain tasks; it's about paying attention to the people that are on each team and how they work together.

When you're in this organizational leadership role, you have to make sure you pay close attention to what's going on in your various teams so that you understand how people work together, and can identify who might be natural leaders, whether they're in positions of leadership at this point in their career or not.

When you have that insight, you can influence teams not only to get the desired output, but also to develop your people and make sure that they're growing from the experience they get from that specific team.

At this level of leadership, you need to understand both your people and your teams deeply to help them thrive. This is when you can set those great expectations for them, and show that you have an even greater heart by offering the support they need to achieve more than they believe possible for themselves.

LEARNING BY DOING

Adults learn best by doing. In the workplace, if you can give someone a project that is not only beneficial to the organization, but also helps them to grow in some capacity, then that's a huge win for everyone.

> *"Situational leadership is a model and a construct where we as leaders let go of control. We learn how and when to let go. We shift our thinking and our approach to draw others into leading themselves."*

One thing that's very important for leadership development is having a formal and recognized way of developing leaders within your company. First of all, your teams need to know that they're part of something bigger, but you also have to show them that there's a pathway to both leadership and growth within your organization.

At PRECorp, we called this our Action-Based Learning (ABL) group. This was the organization's leadership development program, and it was where we trained successful team leaders to grow their perspective of the company. The aim was for them to see the bigger picture of the organization as a whole, and this was where the concept of cross-functional collaboration moved to the next level and helped people grow along the way.

Anyone on PRECorp's executive team could recommend people to be part of the ABL group, and people could also apply directly to join it. When I was CEO, we would try to get a team of six to eight together each time the program started, because we found this was the sweet spot for this kind of team. These people came from across the organization; we had engineers, people from administration, finance, and IT, as well as people who worked in the field directly with the infrastructure.

We carried out leadership assessments to decide who to put on the team. These assessments covered intelligence; how they handled conflict; how they thought; and, one of the most important factors, their abilities to deal with complexity and how far they could envision into the future.

We brought this team together and asked them to work on one of the big challenges that the company was facing. The problems we gave them to solve were the kinds of problems that are the most challenging for any company, because they don't have a right or wrong answer. We gave this team one year to work on that specific challenge and we turned them loose on it.

At the end of the year, we had a formal recognition of the end of the program and recognized what they had achieved. At PRECorp, we found that this process was not only incredibly successful at developing our people, but also at getting them ready to lead multiple teams.

DELEGATING

At an organizational level, delegating refers to what I've just been talking about; namely, how to manage all the teams within your organization and get the best from them. This process also involves elements of monitoring and coordinating, which I'll discuss in more detail shortly.

One thing that you have to become very comfortable with when you're leading multiple teams is letting go. This doesn't mean that you don't care where things go, or that you disconnect, but that you trust your people to take care of things.

This can be challenging if you've been used to focusing on leading a single team. When you're just leading one team, you're very hands-on, you're involved in problem solving, and you're interfacing with people. When you step up to the next level of leadership, the worst thing you can do is dive in and get in the weeds with people, because then you're taking over.

You have to imagine it as though you're in a car with four people, and all of a sudden you open the door, push the person who's behind the wheel out into the street, and start driving. If you do that, everyone else in that car is going to start freaking out. It's the same when you're moving from leading one team to leading multiple teams at an organizational level. You have to be comfortable with allowing someone else to be at the wheel. Or, in this case, turning over control to your teams.

When you start this process of delegating, what really helps is that you've done the work I've already talked about—in terms of putting together teams that work, and making sure that they have team charters and know their purpose.

When you start leading multiple teams, you cease to be a player and you move to the sidelines. Your teams might have problems from time to time, but you have to resist the temptation to jump in and tell everyone how to fix them, even though you might know how.

Instead, you have to coach and guide from the sidelines. You have to tell those people how proud you are of them and how excited you are to see them working on the issues that they're facing. Demonstrating confidence in your teams and their abilities is much more powerful than going in and dealing with issues yourself. It's all part of setting those great expectations and putting trust in people to meet them.

As a leader, you have to be there when your teams need support, which means you ask them questions and help them clarify their thinking. But the key with delegating at this level is to keep some distance, so you're not involved in solving the day-to-day problems. This leads into another element that's important in terms of influencing teams, which is monitoring.

MONITORING

There are several ways you can monitor your teams. The most obvious is looking at a team's output and the results they produce. While that's important, monitoring in the context that I'm talking about is more about paying attention to the people on your teams. It's asking them how they are progressing and having frequent conversations with people.

Think back to the driving analogy earlier in the chapter. You're not wresting the steering wheel from someone else's hands, but you're making sure they know that you're there to support them if they need it. In doing so, you're focusing on leading with self-awareness and empathy to get the best out of your people.

Putting your energy into the people side of your teams is essential if you want to form high-performing teams within your organization. Your focus needs to be on growing people and influencing their strengths, rather than on the figures or targets. Everybody knows what those are, but what you often can't see so easily is what's happening behind the scenes, what challenges people are facing, and how they work together as a team. This is why monitoring those elements of your teams is so important.

From my perspective, at this level, a leader's job is to serve their team and serve their people. You're there to support their efforts; you're not at the center of the effort. When you think about it in this way, it's clear that monitoring isn't about checking up on your teams. The idea is to use the lightest touch possible to get the most amount of insight into how each team is working. The lighter the touch in this area the better, because the heavier your touch, the more you begin to look like you're the one driving the car.

MIKE'S LEADERSHIP LESSON: STEPPING OFF THE MOUNTAIN

Strategy has always been something that's been very important to me and, over the years, strategy and vision are areas in which I've become very good. The problem is, when you're good at something, this is often what you love to do; but if you do all of that yourself, you may be neglecting and underutilizing the rest of the team.

When I first started as a CEO, I wasn't involving the entire team in developing strategy. Instead, I would spend time in my office with maybe one or two other people working on strategy. We'd come up with a great strategy, but then we had to come out of the office, step off our mountain so to speak, and share that strategy with everyone else. People were supportive and gracious, but they couldn't own it, because it wasn't theirs. When you work like this, you may, like me, wonder why your teams don't follow through with the strategy or why people struggle with its ownership.

So we decided to break this model. To do that, we turned over the entire strategy development to a series of cross-functional teams within the organization. This meant we essentially involved half the company in developing the strategy. We used the model of scenario planning in this exercise, which meant that we set out a potential future and three or four future scenarios. Each of the teams took a scenario to work on.

These scenarios were narrative stories about a possible future for the company. Each team was given complete freedom to develop what their scenario looked like. As CEO, I even delegated the development of the scenarios to my executive staff. Of course, I was coaching them along the way and guiding them, but I wasn't in control of the scenarios they developed. That was pretty scary because I had no idea where it was going.

Each member of my executive team then took a particular scenario, formed a cross-functional team, and led the team as they worked on that scenario. All of this took the best part of a year. At the end of that period, their job was to paint a picture around the framework of the scenario they had been given to work with.

I didn't know how they would do that or what they would come back with. Each team produced a video that was about 45 minutes long. These videos included scenes that they'd acted out, mock interviews, clips, and news that were compelling in their scenario.

We watched these videos together once they were completed, and we were able to see the future of our company in the various scenarios. After seeing those videos, we collectively decided which future we wanted to pursue as a company. It was pretty obvious which one we all wanted, and we decided that this would be the basis of our strategy moving forward.

Leadership Lessons . . .

The first step in this process involved me handing over the reins to my executive team, which empowered them. This empowerment filtered down through the entire organization.

When you do this, you have to put up with being in an uncomfortable situation for a while. You might feel frightened that you're not in control, but when you have the courage to turn your teams loose to do the work, you will get incredible passion and buy-in from them.

The output we ended up with from the exercise I described above was amazing. When we decided to translate one of those scenarios into our strategy, everyone at the company bought into it 100 percent, because not only did we have half the people within the organization directly working on the scenarios, they also spent a lot of time telling their coworkers what they were doing and how cool it was. That meant everybody saw what was going on and, by the time we got to the point of using those scenarios to crystallize the company's vision and how we would go about executing that strategy, everyone was already on board.

The interesting thing about this example is that the purpose of what we did wasn't actually as much about strategy as it was about developing people. My aim was to find a way to develop my people and to develop Leaders Worth Following. The project I picked to do that through was turning over the development strategy to the organization teams, instead of keeping it with us few individuals on the executive team.

When you empower your people, you'll have even greater success and get even more satisfaction from your employees, while at the same time taking yourself to a different level. Releasing that control can be scary, but it also leads to incredible results for everyone.

As a leader, you should be aware of your ego and how it may make you hold onto control; and you need to have the confidence in your teams to set aside your ego and allow them to take the reins. Have great expectations for people and give them an opportunity to live up to those expectations, but do so while showing that you are still present to offer support if needed.

BECOME THE CONDUCTOR RATHER THAN PLAYING IN THE ORCHESTRA

Think of an orchestra. Everybody in the orchestra has their instrument and you have groups of instruments within the orchestra. The conductor stands at the front, where they're conducting the music, maybe pulling more from the strings or more from the brass. They're controlling the tempo and adjusting the musicians to get what they want out of the performance.

The conductor doesn't go into the orchestra, grab an instrument from somebody, and show them how to play it. When you're leveling up, from a leadership perspective, see yourself as the conductor. Obviously, everybody has to be playing off the same sheet of music, and it's your job as the conductor to make sure the musicians have the right music. But you're not using an instrument to create the sound. Instead, it's your job to pull all of those different pieces together to create the sound that you want for a particular performance. You're coordinating all the individuals and teams across your organization to arrive at an end result you all envision. This is a perfect analogy for leveraging teams.

THINKING BEYOND YOURSELF

The concepts I've talked about in this chapter are about your vision as a leader and how you see your place in the world. This is about thinking beyond yourself and seeing the awesomeness in and potential of other people.

> *"If we are going to reach our potential as leaders, we need to find the courage to change."*

In the early days of my time as CEO, I certainly had the tendency to try and grab the wheel from my staff but they called me out on it. You can see the payoff from me truly relinquishing control to them in the story I shared earlier in this chapter.

In addition to the amazing product that we got out of asking teams to think organizationally, how I saw my worth as a leader also changed. Before this exercise, I saw my worth as a leader as being the smartest person in a room filled with the smartest people. I determined my worth as a leader based on knowing all the answers and being able to make all the decisions.

When I let go of that control, I had to find my worth as a leader in a completely different way. Now, I find developing people and helping them to grow and become the best versions of themselves, both at work and in their personal lives, to be much more satisfying than being the smartest guy in the room (or thinking that I'm the smartest guy in the room).

CHAPTER 11

ORGANIZATIONAL THINKING

"To be an effective leader, you have to be able to project your vision forward for multiple years, especially in this era when the world is changing quickly."

As we've progressed through this book, we started by exploring the concept of leading yourself before moving toward leading others in the form of teams. As we get to these higher levels of leadership, it's time to frame your thoughts for thinking organizationally.

When you are thinking organizationally, recognize that an organization is much greater than the sum of its parts. The process of organizational thinking encompasses several elements. On one level, it's about watching what's happening within your organization and within your teams. On another level, it's the concept of imagining the various futures for your organization to help you understand what you'll have to deal with.

This is much more than simply looking back at the last year of activity within your organization and trying to extrapolate that to predict what the next year will look like. What I'm talking about is understanding how your organization fits into the overall landscape of everything that's around you. This goes beyond a business and product sense. Look at what's happening in the world around your organization and examine how those things are having an effect.

You might think of this as seeing the big picture, which is part of it, but it's also about visualizing what happens to your organization under future scenarios. These scenarios aren't necessarily predicted through your previous performance; they can be caused by things happening outside your organization.

To me, that's the key to organizational thinking: being able to see how the environment might be putting pressure on your organization, not just this week and not just next week but, in some cases, years into the future.

To be an effective leader, you should project your vision out for multiple years, especially these days when the world is changing so quickly.

TAKING ORGANIZATIONAL THINKING BEYOND YOU

Taking that vision and strategic thinking beyond the CEO's office is particularly important in this context. If all the visioning and strategic thinking at an organization happens only in the CEO's office, then it will only be as good as the CEO.

Sometimes that will be adequate; it might even result in a good plan. The challenge comes when you try to move your organization in that direction. If the visioning and strategic thinking at your organization comes only from you and nobody else, then you have to translate that to the rest of your organization. That will take a lot of time and energy.

What you are aiming for, with your visioning and strategic thinking, is creating strategic alignment within your organization. That means everything and everyone in your organization aligns and focuses on the vision of where the organization needs to go and how it needs to get there. In an ideal world, the people on the front line of your organization will have a clear line of sight for what they're doing and how that affects the vision of the company.

If you can create that line of sight so that every person in your organization knows how they contribute to the overall vision and strategy of the organization, then they become empowered to achieve it and they'll help you move that strategy forward. However, when you create that strategy alone and then try to deliver it to the masses from on high, you give yourself a ton of work to do.

What helps with visioning is to think about your organization in terms of the relationships and people who do different things within it. As a leader, think about how you can align all those conversations and actions; and getting everyone involved from the ground level up helps, as demonstrated in the story I shared in the last chapter.

 ## MIKE'S LEADERSHIP LESSON: STRATEGIC ALIGNMENT

When I was completing my MBA, one of the projects we covered was the process of creating strategic alignment in the organization. For this project, I easily spent 100 hours putting together a mind map that showed all the links between the departments and the people, and how they could be aligned by performance, communication, and even messaging to our members. I was so proud of myself.

I brought this model of how to create strategic alignment within the organization back to my staff and sat down with them to explain the model. Everybody was polite, as they typically are when a CEO comes down from on high and pontificates, and they tried to embrace it and make it work. We had varying levels of success, depending on people's ability to understand the complexity of where things were going and how they were related.

We spent two years trying to align the company to this strategy, but we could never quite get it to work in the way I wanted it to. At the time, I was pretty frustrated and I stepped back from that approach to find a new way forward. I told you about this project in Chapter 10, where I handed over the scenario planning to my teams.

As you saw in the last chapter, that approach was incredibly successful and resulted in tremendous buy-in across the organization.

Leadership Lessons . . .

Strategy consultants will tell you that strategy is everyone's business. What they won't tell you, however, is that if you want it to be everyone's business, it has to be their business from day one.

This was what we achieved by using cross-functional teams to carry out the scenario planning and then used this to inform our strategy for the future. We also found a way that everyone in the organization could be involved in creating that future vision for our company. We did that by setting up a virtual data center and encouraging everyone to contribute to it.

As a leader, you need to see when your approach isn't working as well as it could be, have the humility to admit this, and then find another better way forward. It's important to let go of

ideas that aren't working for the team, even ones that you're in love with. Face reality and know when it's time to ask for help from others.

INVOLVING EVERYONE IN LANDSCAPE ANALYSIS

As I mentioned, we set up a data center with the idea that anyone in the company could add relevant articles or information. In our case, that meant anything to do with energy, Wyoming, and regulations that could impact the business, among others.

As well as pushing this out to our entire team, we also invited people outside the organization to help us create this huge data center. While we were collecting data, a team of people labeled articles and added metadata so we could easily sort all this collected information.

After a few weeks of collecting data, we parsed it down into themes. Once we had those, we asked people to take a deep dive into these articles and create summaries and takeaways. This is what we call landscape analysis.

The result was that, among about 50 people within the organization, we had a pretty clear idea of both the current and future landscapes of the energy industry. Using all the threads of information that we'd pulled together in our data center, we created a tapestry of what our industry's future environment was likely to look like.

At this point, we brought everybody together and started exploring various "What if?" scenarios. This was an exercise we had carried out around ten years previously, and one of the major questions we asked ourselves then was, "What if the energy pivots away from hydrocarbon energy? How will that affect us?"

In our position, that was a pretty scary scenario because PRECorp is a co-op. Co-ops nationally are very heavily invested in the use of coal because, around 50 years ago, whenever co-ops were starting to build power supply, it was illegal in the US to use natural gas to generate electricity. At that time, there were concerns we'd run out of natural gas, which was needed to heat homes.

As a result, co-ops across the US invested heavily in coal. A lot of that infrastructure was in the co-op's portfolio, so imagining what happened when that went away was scary. Through our scenarios, we forced ourselves to consider what would happen if we were no longer using coal and, if you fast forward to today, you can see that coal use is dropping off extremely fast. There are even discussions globally about peak oil demand having been reached, and we saw that in 2020, with people moving away from driving and traveling, in general.

We started imagining this future way back in 2012–13, and we were asking ourselves, "If that future is going to come, what are some of the things we need to do to be ready for it?"

Another scenario we looked at was a high penetration of electric cars and what we would need to do to meet that scenario. We also considered fires and how we would deal with a big fire running through our system, as well as what we would have to do to be ready for that possibility.

PULLING OUT THE COMMON THREADS

Those are just a few examples of the scenarios that we used in our vision. From this exercise, we were left with a list of all the things we could do. At this point, we stepped back and asked, "What are the common steps we, as a company, need to be taking, no matter what happens to us under these scenarios?"

Those common threads highlighted the competencies we needed, the actions we needed to take, and the procedures and processes we needed to be working on to ensure we were resilient and able to deal with any one of those numerous scenarios that could come down the pipe.

These common elements became our strategy for how to have a good company going forward. They informed our vision and helped us to adjust our purpose to enable us to be successful in the future.

The ideas of developing and growing our leadership, as well as focusing on our culture, were the common elements we saw as being essential to the future of the company. One of the most important was having good leadership in the company.

We wanted to have leaders who were comfortable in uncertainty, as well as leaders who were very self-aware, not only in terms of understanding their own performance, but also in how they affected the people around them. These were essentially the cornerstones of our visioning and strategic thinking activity.

Because we had involved so many people from across the company from the beginning, when we began the process of rolling out and formally developing our strategy and its supporting mechanisms, everybody already knew about it. We didn't have to spend time and energy bringing them to where we were or asking them to trust us. Instead, they were already there and actually anxiously awaited the outcomes of our strategic planning and thinking process to enable them to start working on our various initiatives.

Through this process, not only did our leaders understand that the organization is bigger than the sum of its parts and the importance of preparing it to respond to an uncertain future, but a large number of our employees also had this understanding. That meant we were able to create buy-in and move things forward pretty quickly. The outcome here, compared to when I came back to the organization with my awesome mind map, was completely different.

HOW TO INVOLVE PEOPLE IN VISIONING AND STRATEGIC THINKING

When you start discussing how you can involve as many people as possible in your organization's strategic thinking and visioning process, your biggest limitation in terms of resources is likely to be time. Ideally, you want to involve as many people as your organization can afford to involve.

You can certainly do that strategically, starting by looking at your high potentials on the frontline, all the way up to the C-suite managers. When you bring these people together and get them to contribute to your strategy process in the way I outlined above, several things happen.

First, you're getting an output in terms of a strategy or a strategy process that you're ready to launch to the wider organization. Second, you're launching this strategy with many supporters already because they've been part of the process from the beginning. Finally, you're developing your people, which is an important by-product of this approach.

Just by virtue of people being part of this process, working together in cross-functional teams, and looking at some of the challenges facing your organization, they're developing their own abilities to think strategically on this organizational level. You've shown you're willing to teach them, and by giving them the gift of a huge amount of professional training, they'll keep giving back to you, because now you have this group of people who understand the bigger picture. As a result, you'll see better leaders coming through your organization in the long run.

DEVELOPING YOUR OWN STRATEGIC THINKING

To start developing your own strategic thinking, it's important to understand what this is, and what isn't. For me, it comes down to understanding the difference between strategic thinking and operational thinking.

Strategic thinking is thinking about things that add new value to the organization or process, whereas operational thinking is preserving the status quo or preserving value. Operational thinking is, of course, important for leaders, but strategic thinking is what you need to move your organization to the next level.

What you'll find the higher you go in an organization's leadership, and the more responsibility you have, is that you'll spend more and more time in this strategic frame of mind: searching for ideas that can create new value for your organization. To do this you have to step outside yourself and step outside your organization.

This is an ongoing process, rather than a one-time event, and understanding that aspect of strategic thinking is hugely important. Ultimately, strategic thinking leads you to strategy and from there you have to execute that strategy, which in itself becomes a process and discipline.

BE FUTURE FOCUSED

One of the most important aspects of strategic thinking is that you're looking to the future. Earlier in the book, I used the analogy of a car and its headlights. When you're a leader at this level of an organization, you need your headlights to be on bright, like when you're driving at night. You're seeing a little bit around the bend and trying to anticipate the potential issues just over the horizon to make sure your organization is ready for them.

The vision you have for the organization is central to this. It's the reason for your company's existence, and it should, therefore, be a focal point that you can use to inspire your company, move your people to understand how their job contributes to that greater purpose, and how they personally add value.

Once your people start to see how their daily work contributes to something bigger than themselves, you have the ability to involve more than just their day-to-day activities. You start to involve their cognitive resources and their passions. At this point, you start to tap into some of their discretionary time, thoughts, and energy, which truly is of great value to the company.

The way that strategic thinking ties into this vision from your perspective is that, while you're giving people this compelling vision that they can identify with and work toward, you also need to break that vision down into what you're going to do to achieve it.

This is your strategy; it's how you're going to get there. Within that strategy, there will be various initiatives that the company will take to deliver that vision and ultimately achieve it.

The idea of strategy needs to be developed and run just like it's project management. You have your vision, you turn that into an executable strategy, and then you execute the strategy. You measure the results and make adjustments where you need to. This is a continuous process.

Where many companies fail is that they produce a strategic plan in a big thick binder that then gets put on a shelf somewhere and forgotten. You don't need a binder for your strategy. It's far more important that you communicate it to people, both to those within your organization and to your vendors and stakeholders. I would advise you to think of your strategy in the terms of a one-page elevator pitch, because in condensing it you can communicate it, engage people with it, and start working on it.

APPLIED ORGANIZATIONAL THINKING

The Background

The Powder River Energy Corporation (PRECorp) is a member-owned electrical cooperative providing service to over 12,000 members in northeastern Wyoming. In 2007, there was a tremendous boom in energy development in the region, which led to the largest increase in demand that PRECorp had ever faced. The challenge was to scale fast enough to meet this demand.

Pain Points

PRECorp struggled to meet this rapid increase in demand. Connections to the grid lagged behind schedule. The company's internal processes were insufficient to meet the high-volume demands and were inconsistent across its three office locations. Employees lacked adequate training and smooth direction from managers. It quickly became apparent that the business needed to adapt its operations to keep up with the changing market.

Solutions

At PRECorp, we chose to use the Palladium Execution Premium Process™ to drive alignment, not only across the organizational business units and offices, but also within our internal teams and external members. The way we approached each of these challenges varied depending on the group we wanted to reach.

▸ *Members:* We focused heavily on communication. This involved producing a monthly newsletter and inviting our members to share their concerns and ask questions about our strategy. These "pain points" were translated into performance measures that we could actively track and improve at PRECorp.

▸ *Offices and business units:* We defined clear, cooperative-wide measures and processes by bringing different departments together to review and discuss the best ways to conduct and measure our various processes. We also identified the strategic measures that are used as part of our Balanced Scorecards (BSC).

▸ *Employees:* We used the BSC and tied individual employee goals and personal development plans to PRECorp objectives. We made it as simple as possible for people to track and review their progress using personal scorecards. We engaged our employees in scenario-planning exercises, and asked them to examine PRECorp's core values from internal, member, and community perspectives.

The Outcomes

▸ PRECorp's customer satisfaction score was 3.6 percent higher than its cooperative peers and 11 percent higher than investor-owned utilities.

▸ There was greater clarity around PRECorp's performance expectations.

▸ In 2013, an average of five personal goals were set per employee.

▶ Performance incentives were linked to both cooperative performance and scores on individual performance reviews.

▶ Employee motivation and strategic understanding was improved.

There were a number of material improvements between 2008 and 2013 as a direct result of this work:

▶ The work order closeout process time decreased 93 percent, from three years to 70 days.

▶ Outage duration (SAIDI) decreased 57 percent, from 200 minutes to 86 minutes.

▶ Construction time frames decreased 69 percent for residential members, and 64 percent for commercial members.

▶ Employee personal scorecard participation and completion increased from 77 percent to 90 percent.

You can read the full case study at: aleaderworthfollowing.com/casestudy

Building on Success

This case study illustrates what was happening at PRECorp in 2008–2013, but fast-forwarding several years, what we learned about strategy and involving your team was very compelling. In 2021, our strategic update at PRECorp included nearly half of our team in developing our future strategy.

As we executed that strategy, one of the things we learned was that everybody in the company had big ownership of the strategy, and we stayed incredibly focused on the strategy throughout the Covid-19 pandemic. At the time of writing the first edition of this book, we had recently completed an employee opinion survey, which found 99 percent of our employees agreed or strongly agreed that they were very clear about their goals and the organizational strategy. This survey also returned a similar overall employee satisfaction score.

What this demonstrates is that there is a great opportunity to align strategy and capture the hearts and minds of your employees by involving them in the early stages of developing your organizational strategy, as deeply as your organization can afford to do so.

CHAPTER 12

THE MAGIC OF THE BOARDROOM

"When you become CEO, it's important to remember that you're the physical embodiment of the board's decision and with that comes awesome responsibilities and amazing opportunities."

In this final chapter of Part 3, I'd like to focus specifically on how CEOs of cooperatives can work more effectively with their boards. Having said that, what I share here has applications for anyone working for a board of directors, be it in a non-profit or a private company. I'll use the term CEO throughout, although in your organization your title could be manager, general manager, or even executive director. Please take CEO as a term that encompasses all of these titles.

One thing to keep in mind throughout this discussion about working with boards is that one of the most, if not *the* most, important decisions a board of directors makes is who they hire as CEO. This is because you, as the CEO, are the walking embodiment of the board's decision. As a result, there is a significant amount of responsibility, not only due to your position but also because how you interact with your team and company, your stakeholders and your board is a reflection of the board's decision and their faith and trust in you. As you read this chapter, I would like you to keep this in mind.

I hope that this chapter will give you some insight into working with boards and that the stories I share are helpful to you on your journey towards becoming A Leader Worth Following.

THE MYSTIQUE OF THE BOARDROOM

In a professional context, my first experience of company boards was quite early in my career through board meetings at the cooperative I worked for. These board meetings typically happened once a month, and on that particular day (and even throughout the week) the whole atmosphere of the organization changed—people dressed in nicer clothes and appeared to be a little more serious in their day-to-day work. As someone new in that organization, it was obvious to me that something important was happening, not only in the boardroom on the "upper" floor, but throughout the whole organization. The whole event was shrouded in a sense of mystique.

This experience gave me a very healthy respect for the boardroom and the board members themselves. I can clearly remember the first day I had the opportunity to go to the "upper" floor at the cooperative headquarters because I had a meeting with one of the senior executives. I can still hear the swish as the elevator doors opened and remember looking out and noticing that the office was furnished a little differently; there was even a distinctive aroma to this important and impressive space. As I stepped out of the elevator, the carpet felt so thick and deep that I imagined it was swelling up around my ankles. I felt honored (and also a little scared) to be walking the hallways where the board of directors and senior executives worked.

This particular day was a pivotal moment in my career. My meeting with the senior executive was successful and, as a result, I was given more responsibility in the work I was doing, which set me on a different and exciting trajectory within that organization and marked the start of my leadership journey.

The sense of mystique surrounding boards is not an uncommon one and, in fact, I believe it's justified because many important decisions and issues are established in boardrooms. As leaders, we should never forget that when the board has convened, all the people on that board are acting as a unified voice to direct the affairs of the cooperative and set policy. It's a special time and a special place.

We should keep this in the back of our mind, no matter how familiar we are with what happens in the boardroom and no matter how long we have been a CEO. It's truly an honor to be in the position to serve a board that, in the case of electric cooperatives, represents the member owners of the organization.

BUILDING RELATIONSHIPS WITH BOARDS

As my career progressed, I had the opportunity to have a presence at board meetings. I watched several CEOs interact with their board members and, of course, watched those board members interact with the CEOs. Through this process, I could see the value in this relationship and worked to understand this relationship between the board and the CEO. I realized that it involved a continual building of trust between both the board and the CEO.

When this relationship is built correctly over time, it has a significant overall benefit for the organization and the service delivered to its members. However, when this relationship isn't built correctly it can lead to growing feelings of mistrust and anxiety. This tone doesn't only extend to the board–CEO relationship; it will find its way throughout the entire organization and affect the way people interact with each other and the leaders within the organization. Therefore, it's critical that the CEO and the board find a way to work together and continually build trust in each other and the organization for the benefit of everyone— employees and the membership.

When you come to work as a CEO at a cooperative, you'll be serving your members by faithfully executing your duties as a CEO. One of those duties is to work well with the board members, and this not only means building a strong relationship with them, but also understanding what they do and their role in your community.

UNDERSTANDING THE ROLE OF THE BOARD OF DIRECTORS

To build this trust as a CEO, you need to understand the role of the board of directors and have a healthy respect for what they bring to the table. In the world of electric cooperatives, board members will often have strong ties to the community, and it is these ties that have established them as community leaders and helped them get elected to a board seat.

However, oftentimes those ties to the community go much deeper than a CEO may realize or understand at first sight. Particularly in small cooperatives and those in rural areas, board members may have been serving for decades. They may have been elected to the board at a young age and, in some cases, could perhaps have been on the board as long as the CEO has been in the cooperative business.

Many board members will therefore have strong and intimate ties to the community and the cooperative's membership. There are usually fairly strong relationships between board members and employees as well, because many of the employees at cooperatives have worked there for many years. Some of the board members and employees may have even grown up together in the town or service territory for the cooperative, which means it has been part of both their and their families' lives. Many of these families have been part of the cooperative for generations.

As a CEO, it is important to be considerate of those relationships because of the potential closeness between the board and the members, as well as between the board and the employees. When a CEO fails to understand and consider these strong, close relationships, opportunities for conflict arise.

The board makes the decision about who to hire as the CEO. Once they have made that decision, they are looking for feedback to validate that decision and to understand whether this was the best decision for the cooperative. When they are looking for this validation, there will more than likely be conversations between the board members and members of the cooperative, as well as between board members and some of the employees.

While this is an opportunity for the board and the CEO to build trust, it is also an opportunity for conflict to arise if the CEO perceives the conversations between employees and board members to violate the chain of command in the organization. If the CEO sees these conversations as a threat, their ego may kick in and the CEO may become defensive. When that happens, the result is typically not a positive trust-building experience.

MIKE'S LEADERSHIP LESSON: NEW KID ON THE BLOCK

When I arrived at PRECorp as their new CEO over 23 years ago, I was figuratively and literally "the new kid on the block." The cooperative was going through a very challenging time, and the board hired me because of my fresh perspective on the issues and my ability to articulate a compelling vision. I also knew some things had to change.

These changes were scary for many people on the PRECorp team at that time. One of my first acts was to commission an employee survey. I will never forget the painful comments from some of the employees, and in particular the one about the company needing a real CEO, not an apprentice CEO, cut pretty deep. I shared these comments with the board, and they supported me as well as challenged me to build the relationships and the trust I needed to be successful.

It also became apparent that employees were expressing concerns to the board, and this was creating some difficulties for everyone. We decided to set some boundaries in how we dealt with this type of dialogue. We wanted the balance between having one's finger on the pulse of the organization and ensuring that dialogue was productive and transparent.

Leadership Lessons . . .

Both myself and the board recognized the value of this dialogue between the board, and the employees at the cooperative, so we didn't try to squash it. Instead, we agreed how best to gather that feedback and how it would be shared with me.

If an employee came to the board with some feedback, the board members would listen carefully to what they had to say and then ask, "Have you talked to Mike about that?" Usually the employee would say "no," and they would be redirected to me. Often that would be done gently with a suggestion like, "The operational stuff is Mike's responsibility, so you need to talk to him about it." They also reassured the employee that this issue was on their radar. One of the board members would then call me to give me a heads-up about the issue I needed to be aware of and to give me time to think about how best to deal with it.

You have to put down your ego in this situation, be vulnerable, and accept feedback, wherever it comes from. Remember that feedback is part of facing reality on your journey in becoming A Leader Worth Following. You also have to be grateful for that feedback and self-aware enough to see how it can help you develop on your leadership journey.

As you can see from my story, to prevent this scenario from occurring, it's important that both the board and the CEO understand their areas of responsibility and the chain of command. As the CEO, you have to look at conversations between employees and board members, not as a threat to you or the chain of command, but as opportunities to gather data and information about the team and then consider how you can use the information to better serve the team, the membership, and the board.

The CEO and board members may need to have some important conversations to reach this level of understanding. Regardless of an individual board member's relationship with an employee or group of employees, when the board is operating as a whole alongside the manager, the outcome will be that these conversations are seen as a unique way to gather input to help make things better, while keeping the chain of command in mind. What you want to avoid are these conversations between board members and employees resulting in the board directing or demanding action from the CEO.

The best method I have seen to ensure these conversations are used constructively is for these interactions to be presented to the board and the CEO as information. Based upon that information, the CEO can take action to address potential issues or to gain greater insight into what may be happening in the organization.

When used in this way, the outcome of having this information is to make the cooperative stronger and better. It also builds trust with the board, because this way of approaching the information demonstrates that the manager is confident enough in what they do that they don't see this dialogue as a threat. It also enables healthy and robust conversations between the manager and the board to ensure that everybody knows their areas of responsibility.

Typically, that will mean the board of directors is setting policy, helping to make important strategic decisions, setting guidelines and boundaries, and then facilitating and supporting the CEO and management team as they execute that strategy within the boundaries of the policies that have been set.

MIKE'S LEADERSHIP LESSON: CREATING A POSITIVE CULTURE OF COMMUNICATION

As I mentioned in the previous story, when I came to PRECorp as CEO, the cooperative was going through some significant growing pains and transitions because of things that occurred prior to my arrival. There had been a merger which, while completed from the perspective of the organizational name, balance sheet, and broader entity, wasn't even close to being completed from the perspective of the two organizations' cultures. As a result, there were some cultural clashes within the organization when I arrived.

Due to the growth the cooperative was experiencing, changes needed to be made quickly because the extensive growth was putting stress on the organization. This was my first CEO position and I wasn't skilled at managing change at this stage in my leadership journey. I'm sad to say I was more inclined to lean towards an authoritarian style of leadership, where I would issue orders and expect people to follow them. This approach created some heartburn and this information was conveyed to the board of directors.

When this feedback was shared with me, my first response was built around ego. I felt threatened by the channel of communication between board members and employees. I had an open-door policy, but at this stage in my career that wasn't working. Looking back, it's obvious why: if people see that as an open door to a lion's den rather than to a safe and comfortable place where they can have an honest conversation and know they have been heard, they won't be inclined to knock on the door, much less walk through it.

Leadership Lessons . . .

My first lesson from this experience is that taking an authoritative approach with people would have been more effective and appropriate, because I would have been more responsive and communicative. I would have expressed empathy and understanding in my conversations and set boundaries and expectations at a high level. An *authoritative approach* is one that has empathy and warmth, as well as clearly defined goals and expectations. In contrast is an *authoritarian approach*, which is when a leader uses their power to drive things. Sometimes we see an authoritarian style manifest as the "it's my way or the highway" approach.

Working through this situation took a lot of growth on my part and some adept coaching from a very skilled board president to help me understand that we would all do much better at handling those conversations if we saw what came out of them as information that we wouldn't otherwise have had and then collectively decided how to act on this information. I was learning to face reality in my new position, and I was able to own my weaknesses. I also accepted that I was the one who had to change my approach.

We created an approach that allowed employees to talk directly to board members, with the understanding that this information would be reported to me and that I could decide how best to act on it. In doing this, we framed it as an exchange of information and were able to stay in alignment with the chain of command when it came to actually changing the organization or moving it forward.

This was an important step that demonstrated how I could continue as the manifestation of the board's decision. As a result, I showed the board, the membership, and the employees that the board's decision to bring me on as CEO was a good one.

It's important to pay attention to the idea of dialogue between board members and employees. Remember that even though you may feel threatened by that dialogue, by approaching it with an open mind and seeing it as an opportunity for growth and overall improvement, you can turn this into a significant asset for the board, yourself as the manager, your employees, and your membership.

THE NATURE OF BOARD-CEO RELATIONSHIPS

The issues I've just discussed relating to communication might be less likely to occur if you are promoted to the position of CEO from within the cooperative where you already work. If this is how you become CEO, chances are that you already have a good relationship with the various board members, and this can certainly make for a smoother transition to this position.

However, even if you are promoted from within your organization rather than joining as CEO from elsewhere, recognize that things are going to change for you as soon as you step into that CEO role. You are no longer a peer within your established peer group. You won't be a peer with your co-workers, and you won't be a peer with the board members. As the old adage goes, "it's lonely at the top." You'll have other close relationships, but they'll be different and that's OK. It's important to be at ease with yourself and the people you lead, and, yes, you are also leading the board to a certain extent. Being at ease doesn't mean being any less respectful to the person or the position or role they have. Just as you will earn a new type of respect from your past peers, you must also keep a special level of respect for board members, no matter how "at ease" you feel. Stay humble, check your ego, and be self-aware.

THE UNIQUE RELATIONSHIP BETWEEN THE BOARD AND THE CEO

As I mentioned earlier, when you become CEO, remember that you are the physical embodiment of the board's decision and with that comes awesome responsibilities and amazing opportunities. It also leads to a unique relationship within an organization. I have seen CEOs who are visibly struggling in their roles, observed their frustration with the board, and seen the board's frustration with their CEO. I can also say that I experienced some similar stress as CEO.

While unique in many ways, the board–CEO relationship is like any other relationship you have in life, whether personal or professional, in that there will always be some type of conflict. It's simply the nature of being human that we don't always agree and see things from the same perspective. We have to learn to be comfortable in conflict and accept that it's a part of leadership and growth. You'll learn that conflict and the related anxiety won't kill you, and if you look at it constructively, it will make you stronger and a better leader.

When thinking about the board–CEO relationship, we need to remember that when decisions are made in the boardroom, they are made by the entire board. While all boards have their own cultures and operate differently, I believe one of the most important skills a board can have is the ability to unite behind a decision. Even though everyone on the board may not have voted for a particular decision, once that decision is made it's the responsibility of all the board members to enforce and support that decision.

Similarly, as the CEO, you have to support the board's decision, even if it's not the one you were hoping to receive. Any time the board makes a decision that the CEO is unable or unwilling to support, it begins to erode the function and quality of the board–CEO relationship. Again, ego can play a part here, especially when the decision that has been made isn't yours. As a CEO, you have to get behind the board's decision and carry it forward as if it were yours.

There are bound to be times when there's a gap between your perspective as the CEO and that of the board. However, one of the things I've learned over the years is that boards process, consume, and act on the information that the CEO and staff provide to them. If the information the board receives is good quality, the outcomes will likely be better;

and if the information they receive is poor quality, the outcomes will reflect that poor quality.

MIKE'S LEADERSHIP LESSON: TRUSTING THE MAGIC OF BOARD DECISION MAKING

Over the years there were a handful of instances where the board's ultimate decision was not one of, or even close to, my recommendations. This will happen to every CEO at some point, and how it's handled will truly define your career. I have seen CEOs use this opportunity to talk with their staff about how badly the board got this one wrong, and I have never seen that scenario work out for the good of the organization or its membership. I believe in the magic of the board decision-making process and the power of the diverse minds, experiences, and intuitions coming together to solve a problem.

When my board turned right, instead of the left I was looking for, more often than not they were right. There were a few times where I struggled with the right turn they took, and in those situations I was able to see that I had failed in giving the board enough good information for them to reach the best decision. In these cases, I assumed responsibility for making a mistake and told the board that I had made a mistake in not communicating and educating them thoroughly on the issue at hand. After assuming personal responsibility, I sought permission to reframe the matter. They always listened and many times they took the turn to the left that I had recommended. We always learned something when this happened and our mutual respect grew.

Leadership Lessons . . .

When you make a recommendation to your board and they go in a different direction, your first reaction will likely be something along the lines of, "I can't believe they did that!"—especially when your ego kicks in. If you sit with that reaction and dwell on it, it creates conflict and that doesn't serve anyone.

In my experience, boards generally get decisions right; you just don't know it at the time. You have to trust in the magic of the boardroom and the diversity and experience of your board members. However, if you reflect on the decision the board made and assume that the magic worked, but you still don't agree with it, then chances are that you didn't provide them with all the information you have on that topic.

At this point, you have to carefully consider everything you know about a topic and what wasn't conveyed to the board. When you figure that out, you can go back to your board, tell them you made a mistake, and then share this additional information with them. When you reframe a decision in this way, oftentimes you'll see a change.

Recognize when you haven't shared all the relevant information with your board, and be humble enough to admit your mistake. Rather than letting your ego kick in, think about what you could have done better. Show them that you're willing to change yourself to ensure such mistakes don't happen again.

Consider good information in terms of junk food versus healthy food. If you're responsible for providing nourishment to somebody, but all you're giving them is junk food, chances are they won't be as healthy as they would be in all aspects of their life if you were providing them with healthy food. Information is food for the board, so if the CEO wants the board to be strategically focused, they need to give the board strategic information that connects the dots on the complex matters at hand.

If, however, the CEO wants the board to have a strategic focus but spends all their time talking about operational issues, then over time that will grow into a larger and larger disconnect. Therefore, it's necessary for the CEO and the board's president to understand and agree where they are going to take the board and how the board is going to participate in the various functions of the cooperative.

Through my experience, I've found that if you want your board to think strategically you should present information to them from a strategic perspective. If you do otherwise and spend all your time talking to your board about operational matters and then ask them to think strategically, you'll run into conflict.

CEOs can often think of strategy as their domain—early in my career I certainly thought this way. I would develop these wonderful strategies about how we could do things and present these strategies to the board of directors. They would bless these strategies, largely because of trust, and I would leave the boardroom with this wonderful strategy and expect the organization to jump right in and begin executing it.

As I explained in Chapter 10, I learned very quickly that this wasn't going to be effective, because while we could all point to a great strategy, its actual execution was not as strong. I realized that I needed to step off my "mountain" and not only involve the board of directors in its creation, but also the employees. This certainly takes a lot of time, but by involving the board, senior management, and a select group of high-potential and capable subject matter expert employees, you'll be able to understand the landscape around you, see more clearly what's happening in your environment, and then figure out potential ways to reframe challenges and turn those into opportunities. From there you can take opportunities and turn them into definite, actionable items.

Doing this collectively and collaboratively at all levels in the organization and growing that into your finished project or product is a fantastic way to involve both the board and your team in your strategy. This means that the strategy you come up with is not the CEO's strategy rendered from a mountaintop, but the company's strategy, and everybody feels that they own a piece of it. In actual fact, everybody does own a piece of it because they've all contributed to its creation.

DIFFERENT LEVELS OF TRUST

Building trust is an important part of the board–CEO relationship, but it's important to recognize that trust can be developed in many different ways. You have blind trust, for example, and in certain situations such as a crisis where you need to make rapid and immediate decisions, blind trust comes in really handy. Use blind trust very sparingly.

Then there's trust based on experience, where you've seen someone get decisions right so you trust them to make the right decisions in the future. To develop this kind of trust, you need to have a history of making good decisions.

However, if you want to build a level of trust that goes even deeper than this and that really gets to the heart of the culture—who we are, why we do what we do, and how we're going to get to where we need to be—you have to involve people foundationally in the process. The way to develop this kind of trust is by building an underlying commonality of your goals, how you look at the world, and how you approach work. This is probably the richest and deepest form of trust you can develop between the board and the CEO, and even between the employees across the whole organization.

When you have this level of trust, everyone understands what's behind the curtain from a fundamental perspective. They may not agree with everything all the time. But if they know what's behind the curtain and why things are getting done, then it establishes a foundation and culture of trust that is far superior to the rate of right decisions versus wrong decisions that you make and even to blind trust that is occasionally needed in certain situations.

MAINTAINING TRUST IN CHALLENGING TIMES

One of the most important and powerful aspects of the board–CEO relationship is what happens when things go wrong, because (unfortunately) things will not always go right. When things are going well, the board–CEO relationship is very easy; it's when things go wrong that the strength of that relationship is truly tested.

As the CEO, there are innumerable opportunities for things to go wrong in your organization. I believe that it's not only the board–CEO relationship that is important in this scenario, but also the relationship between the CEO and the wider team. The CEO has to assume responsibility for everything that happens in the organization, good and bad. The CEO should step up when things go wrong and take responsibility for what went wrong, rather than throwing someone else under the bus. You can't point fingers or lay blame. Instead, recognize the problem, accept responsibility for what happened, and show the board that you have a plan to correct the situation and ensure that whatever has gone wrong won't happen again. This is all part of becoming A Leader Worth Following.

I'm not going to pretend this is easy. In fact, it's very difficult to stand before a group of people, explain what happened, take personal responsibility, apologize, and then make it right.

MIKE'S LEADERSHIP LESSON: OPERATOR, WE HAVE A PROBLEM

"Mike, we've had a cybersecurity breach, it's our telephone system."

"What's happened?"

"Someone has hijacked the system and gained internal access to our telephone switch. They've harnessed our network of outgoing lines, and we think they're making toll calls."

"How long have they had access?"

"We're not sure, but we're working on shutting the whole system down."

The hackers had access to our phone system at PRECorp for 24 hours during this incident, during which time they made calls to an offshore number and ran up fraudulent toll charges in excess of seven figures. Fortunately, no member data was involved in this breach and I'm happy to say that we arrived at a successful resolution of those charges with our provider.

However, as the CEO it was my job to report this breach to the board and to explain what had happened. A failure to implement some fairly simple safeguards caused the breach of our phone system. I could have easily blamed somebody else for this situation.

Instead, I stood in the breach and accepted responsibility for that seven-figure charge. I told the board that I was aware of our phone system's issues and capabilities. I acknowledged that it would have been an easy question to ask if we were implementing the necessary safeguards. By assuming responsibility for this failure, I shifted the conversation from being about who we were going to blame and the consequences of the mistake to how we would fix things and ensure this wouldn't happen again.

The outcome was that the board and staff sat down together to discuss this particular issue as well as cyber security in general. Ultimately this conversation resulted in our board having an increased sensitivity and heightened awareness of risk vulnerability in relation to our IT and cyber assets. Using this knowledge and working together, we were able to come up with not only a strategy for our phone system, but also an overall cyber security strategy that was many years ahead of its time. We created a position within the organization to manage cyber security, and we also developed a company program to educate everyone about cyber security, monitor potential risks, and to implement corrective action.

All things considered, this story ended well. We learned a valuable lesson and we were able to use this situation to launch a best-in-class cyber security program at PRECorp. This program has been in place for many years now, and I'm proud to say that when I stepped down as CEO, we had reached a level of maturity that was far ahead of other organizations of a similar size, in the cooperative world, in relation to how we managed our cyber security.

Leadership Lessons . . .

If I had gone to the lowest common denominator and laid the blame for this incident on somebody else, I would have turned the conversation with my board into one focused on blame and consequence. By accepting responsibility myself, and promising the board that we wouldn't let this happen again, we moved the conversation toward more constructive outcomes.

In addition, everybody under me who perhaps shared responsibility for that particular breach became even more motivated to support what we were doing and prevent something similar from happening again. What could have been an ugly mess in the organization turned into a unifying cry, supported by the board of directors with the resources we needed to help establish a best-in-class cyber security program.

The ability to stand up and take responsibility is certainly easier when you have a high-trust relationship with your board. The way I think of it is that, as a CEO, you put relationship capital in the bank with the board by being reliable, trustworthy, open, and transparent, and not shying away from having difficult conversations. All of these things add capital to your relationship bank, and this gives you the confidence to stand in the breach and do the right thing for the organization and its membership whenever a big event like this occurs.

By being aware not only of yourself, but also of your relationship with your board and your team, you'll find it easier to follow the right course of action and take responsibility when necessary. To do this with confidence, you need to put capital in your relationship bank with your board.

KEEPING IT FRESH

When I first joined PRECorp I thought I would be there for five to seven years. One of my most influential mentors, Doug Bursey, had told me that managers that stay too long get complacent and eventually the organization ends up serving them, instead of them serving the organization. I understood what Doug was saying, and I also wondered how I would be able to "keep the pace" much beyond that seven-year time-frame. At the end of the first seven years we had harvested much of the low-hanging fruit, and the challenges and opportunities before us would require some very deep digging into the fabric and culture of the organization in order to be addressed.

I had survived the first seven years with tenacity, relentless energy, and too much of an authoritarian leadership style. I think Doug's advice about moving on after five to seven years was grounded on the experience that, by seven years the manager had done all the things they were good at, they had leveraged their strengths, made a difference, and now it was time for another skill set to come in and do the same.

I spoke with my board about this and also expressed a desire to reinvent myself and to consider letting go of those things that had helped me be successful so far. I explained that I thought these very things were also what was holding me back from serving the organization and its membership at an even higher level, and these could be things that might limit our future success. I asked the board to support my pursuit of an MBA and they agreed. This MBA was unique in that it focused on servant leadership development in addition to business principles and strategy. I committed to another five years at PRECorp in order to have the company invest in supporting me in this program.

It might have been easier to follow Doug's plan, but the board had faith in me, and the collective wisdom of the board realized that by focusing on servant leadership, we could effectively dive into the toughest issues we were struggling with. As I look back today after a 23-year career at PRECorp, the MBA was the first of many reinventions of myself. It showed me how I could be a more effective leader. Each of these steps was supported and encouraged through ongoing dialogue and feedback with the board. The board embraced the idea of annual CEO 360 evaluations as well as annual Employee Opinion Surveys and the results and trends of this helped us keep it fresh. We didn't shy away from feedback and self-reflection, and we built a mutual respect while maintaining a sense of ease.

Working with your board is a key part of your job and your opportunity for growth. My suggestions are to be open, transparent, and honest. Make feedback a welcome addition to all your conversations. Establish and respect boundaries, the varying roles of the players, and the awesome magic of the boardroom process. Give your board good information and help them focus on what matters most.

Never forget that you are the embodiment of their most important decision.

BECOMING A LEADER WORTH FOLLOWING

PART 4

TOOLS TO SUPPORT YOUR LEADERSHIP JOURNEY

Now that we've explored the three stages of the leadership continuum and looked at how choosing the path to becoming A Leader Worth Following can help you thrive at each stage, I'd like to share some tools that I believe are particularly helpful to all who embark on this journey of continuous development and self-improvement as a leader.

The first tools are motivational interviewing and active listening. I've already touched on active listening earlier in the book, but in Chapter 13 I take a deeper dive into what this means and how you can use this approach in your interactions. Motivational interviewing is an incredibly powerful technique that I learned of through my studies in mental health counseling, but to harness its true power, you also need to master active listening.

In Chapter 14, I will share the three No-Os of leadership—ego, dinero, and libido—and explain how you can use this concept to check your decision making and actions as a leader. Briefly described:

▸ **Ego**—If a leader makes a decision out of ego, that decision will typically put the leader at the center of it. An ego-based decision isn't looking out for, or serving, the organization and is all about the leader, which doesn't work well. True leadership is a desire to serve, not to be served.

▸ **Dinero**—A decision driven by dinero is one that's serving the leader financially. The important question here is, "Is there a financial or other reward to me personally by making this decision that is hidden and not a normal part of performance compensation?" Again, any decision made based on dinero usually doesn't work well for the organization or the team.

▸ **Libido**—This can be thought of as decisions to engage in inappropriate relationships in the workplace. But if you scale it up, libido is about a leader using their power inappropriately, often to disempower others. Checking your decisions against libido is about making sure there isn't an attraction to something or someone that's driving your decision.

I like to think of these three things as leadership landmines, and my hope is that by making you aware of them you're able to sidestep them on your journey to becoming A Leader Worth Following. Ultimately, if you look at some of the epic leadership failures out there, you can see that this trifecta of ego, dinero, and libido have gone awry in the decision-making process.

In the final chapter of Part 4, I encourage you to consider your own self-care. As leaders at any stage of our journey, we need to take care of ourselves in order to be able to take care of others. Self-care can be a challenging concept to nail down, as everyone has different activities that work for them. To make it easier to apply to your life, I've broken self-care into six dimensions that I believe we each need to hit every day in order to live well.

These six dimensions are social, spiritual, physical, occupational, organizational, and emotional. If you truly desire to embark on the journey to becoming A Leader Worth Following, you must learn to care for yourself so that you can care for and be of service to others. By creating your own daily practice that encompasses these six elements, you can ensure you are bringing your best self to all of your interactions, both professional and personal.

CHAPTER 13

ACTIVE LISTENING AND MOTIVATIONAL INTERVIEWING

"As A Leader Worth Following, your role is to help team members recognize the need to change, not to force change upon them"

As you know, changing yourself first is one of the core elements of becoming A Leader Worth Following. Of course, being a leader involves helping the others you work with recognize when they need to change, and helping them make those changes to benefit both themselves and the wider organization or team. This is easier said than done. However, in my training as a counselor I have uncovered a very valuable technique to help people change by encouraging them to talk about that change— motivational interviewing. This technique can be just as easily applied to leadership as it can to counseling.

Motivational interviewing was first developed by William Miller for counselors to use with those struggling with substance abuse. He then worked with Stephen Rollnick to refine the technique, which is when it became known as motivational interviewing.

The primary aim of this technique is to guide someone else through the stages of change, ultimately reaching a place at which they feel equipped to take action and make the necessary change in their lives. The five stages of change as set out under the motivational interviewing framework are:

Stage one: Precontemplation

Stage two: Contemplation

Stage three: Planning

Stage four: Action

Stage five: Maintenance

What I have observed, both through my work in counseling and leadership, is that doing everything for someone else doesn't actually help them in the long term, even though you might feel as though you're being helpful in the moment. In fact, what you're doing is hurting the other person's sense of agency and autonomy. The key is to help other people take action for themselves. Just as you have to change yourself first, so too do others. As A Leader Worth Following, your role is to help them recognize the need to change, not to force change upon them.

It's worth remembering that models such as this one are always more simplistic than the situations you experience in real life. The purpose of the motivational interviewing model, and others like it, is to help us wrap our heads around something that is very complex. While I believe this is an incredibly useful technique to use with those you lead, it can also be helpful to have the self-awareness to apply this to yourself. For the purposes of this book, I'll run through the technique as though you are working through it with another person, because this is where it is most effective.

STAGE ONE: PRECONTEMPLATION

Many times, people don't know that they need to change something—this can also be true of us as leaders. So, in the precontemplation stage, you may be dealing with someone who has a feeling that something isn't quite right, but they can't put their finger on what that is. Or you could face a stronger reaction, such as an outright denial that something needs to change. The person you're talking to may not want to see what could be obvious to others. In other cases, you'll be working with someone who wants to change, but who needs support to do so.

The ultimate aim at the end of the precontemplation stage is for the other person to recognize that there is a need for change, and for them to start thinking about how that change could be beneficial for them.

To help them reach this point, focus on developing what's known as discrepancy, which is when the other person is also able to understand that something about their current behavior or situation isn't right. If that person has come to you with a nagging feeling that something isn't quite right, they're already on this path.

For those who deny that there is a need for them to change, begin guiding them towards this discrepancy by asking open-ended, leading questions. For the purposes of this example, let's say the person we're talking to has come with a problem relating to presenting in meetings, but won't acknowledge their own part in creating this problem. Your dialogue could go something like this:

You: "Could you tell me about a time when maybe this wasn't a problem?"

Them: "Okay, yeah, well there was this one meeting where I gave a presentation, and I felt like I communicated really well. It all went really smoothly and I felt really great."

You: "So what was different about that situation to the one you have now?"

Them: "I guess I'd had a really good night's rest and I felt really well prepared for that presentation, because I'd put so much work into it beforehand."

You: "So what are some things that you think you could do differently in future, to get back to being able to deliver great presentations?"

Essentially by using these open-ended questions, you're encouraging the other person to reflect on what's happened and realize that they have the power to influence the outcome, but in order to do so, they need to make a change.

When you're asking these questions and working towards developing discrepancy, it's vital that you're practicing active listening, which I touched on in Chapter 6, and which I'll come back to in more detail shortly. When you do so, you are fully present with the person in front of you; you're warm, engaged, and making eye contact with them. You're using non-verbal communication cues to show them that you are listening and that they've been heard. You want to get to a place where you're activating the mirror neurons I mentioned in Chapter 1, which means you're in tune with the other person and feeling what they're feeling. You're relying on your empathy as a leader to guide this conversation and show the other person that you truly care about them.

Of course, even if you do all this, you may still encounter some resistance. That resistance might be obvious, like someone saying, "Hell no, I'm not doing that!", or it could be more passive. Look for cues that the person you're talking to is cutting themselves off—maybe they adopt a defensive position with their body, such as crossing their arms or leaning away from you. Maybe they go quiet and stop fully engaging with the conversation.

When we encounter resistance, the temptation can be to push harder. However, becoming more forceful rarely works. Instead, a better approach is to reframe that resistance as something you need to overcome—do you need to adapt your communication style? Are your probing questions a little too much? Could you be warmer and more empathetic? Perhaps you simply need a break to check-in with the other person.

If you decide to pause and check in, the best way to do so is to ask permission before you ask if the other person is doing OK. So you might say, "Hey, I've got a weird feeling, so is it OK if I ask you a question about how you're doing right now?" Once the other person gives you permission to continue, you can then say something like: "Well, we've talked a lot about this and it might sound hard and scary, so I'm just wondering how you're doing with this conversation? Are you OK?"

Once they've answered, you can get back into the flow of the dialogue or, depending on their answer, you may decide it's time to park the conversation for now. Asking permission *before* you ask how they're doing is the key though, because in doing so you're creating safety for the other person and putting them in control.

One of the fallacies of leadership is thinking that you are in control all the time, but there is a lot of benefit to letting go of that control, provided you see that things are moving in the proper direction.

As you begin to see discrepancy developing, you can move out of the precontemplation stage by summarizing the conversation so far: "This all sounds really great. What do you think would happen if you started doing that?" This is when, the conversation having gone well, the other person will realize that they need to make a change.

Precontemplation: Develop discrepancy by asking probing questions, being attentive to the other person's feelings, and helping them move towards an "A-ha!" moment.

STAGE TWO: CONTEMPLATION

When the other person has recognized that they need to make a change, your role is to help them see how that could look and how it will benefit them as well as others around them. As you move into contemplation, you want them to contrast how things could be different if they take the action they've identified. You also want them to explore the advantages and disadvantages of doing so.

By examining these questions, you help the other person understand the value proposition around the change and why it may be important to them. Again, use open-ended questions to get the dialogue flowing and keep it moving.

One of my favorite questions within the contemplation stage is what's known as a scaling question, where you ask the person to give their suggestion a rating out of ten. Let's imagine someone has come to you and said that they feel they could perform better in their role if their team would do *X*.

You could say, "That's a great idea. I'd like to ask you a question about that . . . On a scale of one to ten, with ten being extremely important and one being not important, how would you rate the importance of making that change for your success?"

Let them answer and then build up to a second scaling question, such as by saying: "It sounds like that change is really important to you because you scored it a seven out of ten, and that's over halfway. So this is something that's really important to you?" The other person will hopefully reply with a "yes," then you can continue: "Can I ask you one more question about this? Could you tell me the likelihood of you being able to do that, with zero being not at all likely and ten being extremely likely?"

This second question can be tricky, because anyone who's authentic isn't going to score themselves a ten—if they did the question would really be, "Why haven't you done this already?" Let's say that in our example, the person you're talking to answers with an eight. This is where you can start to move them toward the third stage of change.

Summarize what they've just told you to help them take another step towards action. So you could say: "Wow, can I just summarize for a second? When we talked about this, you said that it was about a seven in terms of importance to you, and the likelihood of you being able to do it was an eight. So I'm just curious: why didn't you score yourself lower?"

This might sound like an odd question to ask, but this is where the magic happens. This is a strengthening question, because when you ask, "Why didn't you score yourself lower?" the other person will focus on the importance of the change, as well as the strengths and abilities they possess to make that change happen. When they articulate this, you can help them move them into the planning stage.

Contemplation: Encourage the person to see how making the change could improve their situation by asking scaling questions and summarizing their answers before asking that all-important strengthening question: "Why didn't you score yourself lower?"

STAGE THREE: PLANNING

Once you've worked through the scaling and strengthening questions in the contemplation stage, summarize what they've told you to set up the planning stage. If we continue with the same example, you could say: "So you told me this change was a seven in terms of its importance, and that it's an eight in terms of you having the strengths to get this done. Do I have that right?"

When they agree, you can move into planning by saying, "Great, so let's talk about how we might do this . . ."

As with the other stages, the idea here is for you to guide the other person towards the answers, rather than telling them what they need to do. With that in mind, a great question to go to next is, "What's the smallest step you can take that will move you in the right direction?" At this point, the conversation will usually turn into a back-and-forth brainstorm as you come up with a plan together. Remember to keep asking open-ended questions, paraphrasing when it's appropriate, and asking probing questions when you feel those will be beneficial.

Probing questions are things like, "You said that this would occur. I'm just curious why you think that?" They are designed to pull a little more detail out of the other person to help ensure the plan they come up with is really robust. If you manage to reach this stage in the course of one conversation (and you may well not—motivational interviewing can take multiple conversations to reach this point), then usually the planning stage is a good point at which to break.

End the conversation with a summary of what you've discussed. Something like the following can work well: "So we've talked about X, you've thought about how this could be an important change for you to make, we've identified your strengths and the things you could do to make this change, and we've identified the smallest step you can take to put you in the direction in which you want to travel. Until we can meet again, why don't you practice that small step, and maybe you can think of other steps you may want to take or things you might want to change and then come up with a plan that we can discuss next time we speak. How does that sound?"

It's important, in motivational interviewing as well as other conversations where you're actively listening, to ask for feedback from the other person. By doing so, you're getting their buy-in, and as a result they're much more likely to follow through by developing a plan and moving into the next stage: action.

Planning: *Use open-ended and probing questions to help the other person develop a plan for achieving the change they want to see. Summarize the key points and give them some "homework" to work on their plan if you need to break the session.*

STAGE FOUR: ACTION

In any plan to change, the first small step is always the hardest one to take. It's too easy to think of making a change as all or nothing—you need to go to the full 100 percent or not bother. But the reality is that taking that first step, and starting that journey towards change, is really what you need to do.

When the person comes to speak to you again, you can review their action plan and go through some of those probing and scaling questions again. Don't forget about developing discrepancy, because this is what helps that individual understand why they want to change; from there, your role is to give them the strength to do what's necessary to make that change by helping them see their own strengths and capabilities. Build their autonomy at every stage.

Action: *Get the other person to identify the one small step they can take that will start their journey towards change. Use probing and scaling questions to review their plan and help them keep moving forward.*

STAGE FIVE: MAINTENANCE

Maintenance is the final stage in motivational interviewing, and it's very important, because this is how you help the other person continue their journey of change. Ask questions like, "What can you do to keep moving in this direction?" or "What can you do to keep *X?*"

An important part of maintenance is keeping the other person engaged with the changes they are making. When you begin this process and help them feel discrepancy, what you're doing is directing their attention to a source of discomfort. As this person begins to take action to change, they close the gap on that discrepancy and it begins to feel more comfortable. This is when it can be easy to stop taking action because everything feels better.

To counter the potential for a loss of momentum, draw their attention to the successes and rewards they've experienced as a result of making that change.

Maintenance: Draw their attention to the successes and rewards they've seen so far to help maintain momentum. Ask probing questions to help them see the path ahead and encourage them to keep taking small actions.

ROLL WITH RESISTANCE

Resistance may come up at various points throughout this process and the key to tackling it is to not push back on it. Instead, you should roll with it. This is much like how you deal with an opponent in martial arts. For example, in judo when an opponent comes at you, you don't try to stop them, you grab them, step back, and redirect their energy in the direction in which you want it to go.

When it comes to resistance, don't meet it head-on. Instead, redirect their energy to help pull the other person in the direction they want to travel. Roll with it and guide them, whether that resistance is coming up in stage one or stage five.

You may encounter resistance that doesn't feel like resistance in the form of overly positive statements. This is particularly the case when it comes to the scaling questions I mentioned in the contemplation stage. Be wary of anyone who scores themselves a ten on the scaling questions—often that can make your job harder! If they really believe they score ten on both of those questions, then ask why they're even talking to you about this problem.

In actual fact, this is a form of resistance by itself, because it often indicates the person is ignoring the problem. Remember that real change isn't effortless; it will always take work. If someone does score themselves as a ten on those scaling questions, get permission to challenge them. Ask if they're OK for you to ask them an honest question, and then go with: "So you've scored yourself a ten in terms of the effect it would have and in terms of you having the ability to make the change, so my question is why is this a challenge? Why isn't this something you've already changed?"

Once you've asked that question, though, you're going to be thinking on your feet, because people are unpredictable. If they maintain that it's easy for them to make the change, suggest that they do just that, and that you'll check in about how it's going in a week or even a few days, depending on what's appropriate. Have that conversation as many times as it takes to move them from contemplation to planning and into action.

Remember that declaring success before the battle is a form of resistance, but as a leader you can't fix it by challenging it head-on. You have to maneuver around it and redirect the other person's energy and thought processes about the change until they arrive where they need to be themselves.

USE ACTIVE LISTENING

I mentioned active listening skills earlier in this chapter and briefly in Chapter 6, but they deserve more of a deep dive because this is an important technique for leaders at all levels to understand and use in their day-to-day interactions with their teams. In fact, it's an essential life skill and practicing active listening will make all of our relationships—personal and professional—better.

However, as leaders we often fall into the trap of thinking that we're so busy we just have to get stuff done. We tend to equate action with success; whereas active listening is about slowing down, holding space, being present, and creating a connection. It doesn't require you to *do* anything. It requires you to pause. But in pausing, you create space to achieve so much more.

Understanding active listening is only half the process. We also need to understand what active listening is not. So, active listening is not problem solving. As leaders we often feel as though we have to fix everything, so when someone comes to us with a challenge, we have to resist the urge to jump into fix-it mode. Other people need to learn to fix things for themselves. Active listening on your part will allow them to do that, but it can be challenging and uncomfortable when you first make a conscious effort to actively listen.

For a start, you need to be engaged. That means you have to quit looking at your phone, stop worrying about your next meeting, and just focus on the person in front of you. Active listening is mostly in your non-verbal cues—it's about the eye contact, your body language like leaning in, subtle movements like nodding, and the odd vocal confirmation, like "Ah ha" or "tell me more," to show that you're still following the conversation.

Eye contact can be a tricky one to get right, and appropriate levels of eye contact will vary between cultures and countries, so be mindful of how eye contact is perceived by the person to whom you're listening. Are they okay with eye contact, or could they find it intimidating or even rude depending on their upbringing and culture?

When you are able to focus on the person in front of you and you're truly present and open with them, you'll feel a connection and they'll feel it, too. You will also start to feel what the other person is feeling—that's your empathy kicking in.

Another way to demonstrate active listening in a conversation is through paraphrasing. However, it's important to remember that paraphrasing isn't just parroting back what the other person has said. Instead, you want to paraphrase in a way that invites further conversation. For example, if someone comes to you and says, "I'm having a really bad day," rather than responding with, "So you're having a bad day?" try replying with, "Oh, you're having a bad day? I hate bad days." This is a subtle difference, but it encourages the other person to keep talking while showing that you understand how they feel. Match their tone with your responses and it will send a signal that you're meeting them where they are.

Summarizing is also useful, particularly if the other person has talked for a little while without interruption. So in the previous scenario, you could say, "It sounds to me like you're having a really tough day and you're really stressed out." When the other person responds to your assessment with an emphatic "Yes!" you know that you've made a connection. When that happens, it feels fantastic.

It can be very easy to isolate ourselves as leaders, and for others to isolate us. When you rise to a certain level of leadership, you may find others put you on a pedestal, and that makes it harder for them to connect with you. However, when you can find moments to create connections with people and let your guard down a little, you'll find that they reciprocate by going the extra mile for you and that's really powerful.

In my experience of people coming into and leaving organizations, they usually leave because of a poor relationship with their supervisor. Conversely, people will stay at an organization for longer, even when things get tough, because of their relationship with their supervisor. Active listening is certainly a leadership skill that pays dividends when you get it right.

BLEND ACTIVE LISTENING AND MOTIVATIONAL INTERVIEWING

Active listening goes hand-in-hand with motivational interviewing, because in order for that technique to be effective, the other person needs to feel heard and feel as though they have a safe space in which to discuss challenges and find potential solutions. More often than not, those solutions will require them to change.

Both of these are skills that anyone aspiring to be A Leader Worth Following would do well to have in their tool kits, because they are so powerful. Active listening, in particular, is invaluable, because when you can connect with people, help them have those "A-ha!" moments, and show that you understand them on a personal level, it's good for the individuals with whom you work, good for the team, and good for the organization.

The aim is to create a safe space for someone where they feel they don't have to be perfect and they can be human. I believe that's one of the biggest gifts we can give our people.

Through both active listening and motivational interviewing, you are also creating connection, which breeds authenticity and trust. When you have that connection with your people, they won't be afraid to tell you the bad stuff, which can only be a good thing because the sooner you know about it, the easier it is for everybody to resolve it.

There are many books out there about creating trust, but I believe that if you focus on developing your active listening skills, then you'll go a long way toward building the trust that's essential for high-performing teams.

Both these techniques support you on your journey to become A Leader Worth Following. Be self-aware in the first instance to recognize how you listen, and identify what you need to change. Own your weaknesses and be prepared to change yourself first to encourage others to do the same. Demonstrate empathy by listening and meeting people where they are, and show your willingness to learn about their experience. Demonstrate your great expectations and even greater heart by helping them solve their own problems, while facing the reality of the situation they present you with. By responding to them in a calm, measured way, you're being emotionally predictable and mentally strong.

This also demonstrates why I believe so strongly in the concept of becoming A Leader Worth Following, because those eight elements naturally encourage you to develop the skills you need to be the best possible leader for your people.

CHAPTER 14

THE NO-Os OF LEADERSHIP

"Being cognizant of the No-Os of leadership and checking your behavior, decision making, and thinking against them will make you a better leader: one who is easier to follow."

Over the course of my professional career, I've had the opportunity to work under many different leaders. At the same time, I've always been a student of leadership and am always working to become a better leader. I've sought to understand what makes good leaders and what makes bad leaders.

I would see leaders that I knew experiencing leadership failures and I would also see leaders who are in the public eye, such as presidents, politicians, and other high-profile figureheads, experiencing leadership failures. One day they would be on top of the world; the next they would be gone. I started observing these leadership failures, being astute, and always seeking to understand what had happened, because I wanted to be a good leader and avoid those kinds of failures.

What came out of this observation isn't a scientific study, but it led me to the No-Os of Leadership. As I said in the introduction to Part 4, these No-Os are ego, dinero, and libido. I believe using them to check your decision making can help you in your quest to become A Leader Worth Following.

I've talked about how important it is for leaders to be self-aware, and whenever I'm coaching leaders and discussing problems and challenges, one of the areas I talk about with them is epic leadership failures. What I've noticed is that, if you're in a situation where one of those No-Os is activated, you're on dangerous ground. These are big red flags that you, as a leader, need to be thinking about and aware of.

EGO FAILURES IN LEADERSHIP

An ego failure in leadership is when a leader is blind to themselves. They make decisions that are all about themselves, not about their people. I'm not saying that good leaders should have no ego, but they should have humility and be humble. If you make a mistake, take responsibility and don't blame other people. Making a mistake and blaming it on everyone else is a clear sign of an ego issue. As Ken Blanchard says: "Great leaders don't think less of themselves, they just think about themselves less."

It boils down to the signals we send to our people. For example, as the leader, do you have the best parking space right by the front door to the building? You may have it for a reason, because you're always coming to work late or you're in and out all the time, but do you always have to park there? And if someone else parks in that space by the front door, do you get mad about it? Do you feel angry or stressed if that happens? Could you instead think, "I'm sure they were in a hurry" or "I need a walk today"? That's just a very small example of how, as a leader, you cannot lead with your ego.

Ego also means being blind to your weaknesses and the overextension of power as a leader. Ego tends to feed and create even more challenges for the No-O of libido, which we'll talk about later. Ego manifests in a lot of ways in leadership; it's an assumption that no matter what you do or think, you're right and that the wake you create through your actions is of no consequence. As you now know, taking this approach will lead you far from the pathway towards becoming A Leader Worth Following.

There are lots of examples of ego failures in politics. In fact, I don't think a person can be a successful politician without having a strong sense of self and a strong ego. However, where I think it can go awry is when politicians and leaders don't pay attention to their wake and the impact of their ego on others.

MIKE'S LEADERSHIP LESSON: ELECTING THE 46TH PRESIDENT OF THE US

On November 3, 2020, U.S. voters went to the polls in what was one of the most anticipated and talked-about presidential elections in recent history. Donald Trump was campaigning for a second term. Joe Biden was the Democratic nominee. In the lead-up to the election, the polls were inconclusive. In the days after the polls closed, there was little else on the news other than which of the candidates had won which states and the associated electoral college votes.

Eventually, Joe Biden was declared the winner and named as the 46th president. But something remarkable happened in the days following the election. Incumbent Donald Trump refused to concede the election. He peddled stories about voter fraud, despite credible evidence to the contrary.

His insistent narrative that the election had been "stolen" from him led to a huge demonstration on January 6, 2021, and the country's Capitol building nearly being overrun as a joint session of Congress met to formalize Joe Biden's election as the U.S. president.

Leadership Lessons...

The group of Trump supporters who gathered at the Capitol that day, intent on disrupting the count of Electoral College votes, were there as a result of Donald Trump's failure to concede the election and his inability to see what the wake of that decision might be. The flip side, of course, is that he was fully aware of his wake and that this was the outcome he intended, which is even worse.

Donald Trump's ego prevented him from accepting that he could be wrong. The resulting wake from his decision can be seen clearly in the images and news reports of what happened that day.

Of course, we'll never know for sure whether Trump conceding the election would have prevented this demonstration and subsequent riot from taking place. However, I think many would argue it would certainly have been a smaller, less-eventful demonstration at the very least had Trump walked away from the White House gracefully, rather than allowing his ego to blind him to the truth of what was happening.

As a leader you have to accept that you can be wrong and, when you are, to be humble enough to take responsibility for that, as well as any outcomes that your wrong decision may have caused.

DINERO FAILURES IN LEADERSHIP

It seems in today's world that money is a huge motivator. One of the things I learned from Ken Blanchard is the concept of the triple bottom line. This refers to happy employees, happy customers, and the revenue that results from both of those things, without being the primary driver. Dinero can show up in how we run and focus our businesses.

We know businesses need to make money to be successful. Dinero isn't about making money in that sense. What I'm talking about is making decisions that are solely intended to benefit you (or the business) from a financial perspective, without consideration of your employees or customers. When that happens, it's a problem.

Dinero failures can also show up in leaders who make decisions to enrich themselves at the expense of their employees and their members or customers. For example, I haven't seen a corporate bankruptcy filing that doesn't give the executive team huge bonuses and a huge payout early on. That's usually explained away by saying that these are key people who are needed to run the organization while it's restructured. However, I tend to think that if leaders have their dinero in check, they would have a sense of responsibility to their employees and their customers, and would therefore feel less entitled to large bonuses when things are going badly, and be more motivated to do the right thing and take care of their employees and customers.

MIKE'S LEADERSHIP LESSON: MONEY TRICKS

Joe was 17 and looking for a job. He found one with Steve, who ran the local auto shop. Although Joe didn't fully understand all the ins and outs of business, one thing he did register about Steve was that he seemed to be more concerned about money than he was about taking care of people and doing the right thing.

Joe quickly learned that if Steve was able to take a used part and make it as good as new, he would charge customers for a new part. The other mechanics used to quietly shake their heads at this practice, but they all needed their jobs so none of them spoke up.

One of the older mechanics even told Joe that Steve didn't use to play these tricks, but that once he had accidentally charged a customer for a new part rather than a used one that had been repaired, and the customer hadn't noticed it. Steve had realized he could make a bit of extra money here and there with this, so instead of seeing it as a one-off occurrence it became a part of his operations.

One day, Steve took Joe to the side and asked him to help catch an error at the bank. He wrote Joe a check for $250 and told him that if he went to the bank and cashed it, he could keep $50 and just give $200 back. This happened reasonably frequently, and it took Joe years before he understood that Steve was actually using him to get money from his operating loans.

The problem was that the more Steve behaved in a shady manner, the more his business struggled and the more he turned to underhanded practices to make up the difference. Like many of the mechanics who worked there, Joe felt uneasy and after a couple of years left for another job. None of them felt as though they could say anything to Steve or stand up to him. Eventually, Steve's auto shop went out of business, despite the fact that he always had good mechanics working for him.

Leadership Lessons . . .

Steve wasn't a bad person, but he didn't always do the right thing and was often motivated to make decisions based on his financial gain, going against the dinero No-O of leadership.

However, his leadership failures started off as small things. In fact, the first time he sold a used part as a new part, it was a mistake.

But Steve never challenged his leadership against the No-Os. He didn't stop to ask whether his decisions were being driven by his own financial gain rather than what was best for his customers. He wasn't transparent about his operations and, ultimately, that resulted in him losing business.

Steve also failed in his leadership in that he put his team in a difficult position where they were unable to stand up to the practices they disagreed with. Throughout my career I have certainly seen people do shady things, and it can be easy to wonder why no one speaks up when you're on the outside looking in. However, it's very difficult to stand up and say something when you are not in a position of power within an organization.

There are also leadership lessons from a self-leadership perspective in Joe and Steve's story. Wherever you are on your leadership journey, it's important to test your decisions against those No-Os of leadership. Ask yourself questions like: "Am I getting a personal reward from this situation?" or "From a monetary perspective, do I have an unfair advantage in this situation?" You may not feel as though you have the power to stand up to poor leadership where you are now, but you can always lead yourself according to those standards. Joe did, which is why he left to find another job.

As leaders, we know that being financially strong is important for any organization, but it's better to approach decision making from the perspective of serving your members or team than purely from financial motives.

When organizations go through financial stress, they'll make budget cuts and other changes. If you, as the leader of the company, aren't leading by example and taking those cuts yourself, whether that's to your bonus or your compensation, then that will create problems because people will find out.

If you're considering pay cuts in your organization, you'd better cut your wages a year before you cut anybody else's, and don't tell anybody about it. That will mean the year that you implement those pay cuts you can say, "I've already been doing this for a year myself." People will respect that.

LIBIDO FAILURES IN LEADERSHIP

As a leader, it's important to understand your relationship with leadership and, in this context, there are three components: passion, commitment, and intimacy. Passion is the internal energy that moves you to seek what you desire. Commitment in this context is in terms of your relationship with yourself as a leader. It's about remembering who you are, what's important to you, and what values you identified in your leadership point of view. Intimacy means knowing yourself and being able to face your weaknesses and identify areas you could improve. This also involves having the willingness and desire to address any faults you see. These three elements—passion, commitment, and intimacy—need to be a balanced triangle.

Libido can be a leadership challenge when the passion side of your relationship with leadership is out of balance. So if you overly focus on passion as a leader and don't balance that with commitment and intimacy, your libido could go unchecked.

If we're honest with ourselves, I think we can agree that we've either experienced or caused other people to experience an unchecked libido in the context of our passion being out of control. Organizationally, I've been in a position where something has upset me and my passion and emotions are heightened. I can remember sitting down early in my career when I was in this state to write the kind of scathing email that puts the other person down and elevates me. Can you identify with this? You hit send, but you don't get to take those emails back. Those emails can be damaging to the individual you send them to and also to your team.

Mostly, when you release that passion into the workplace without carefully considering the message that you're sending, the position that you're taking, and how you're using your power as a leader, what you're really doing is setting an example of what happens when you have an unchecked libido, which has no place in the workplace.

When you look at the leadership failures that result from when that passion becomes sexual in nature, those are often what could be described as epic leadership failures. I'm not trying to make a moral statement with the idea of libido, but if you look at the disruption that happens in an organization when a leader has an unchecked libido, it's pretty crazy.

In 2009, there was a news story about the governor of South Carolina going missing. For six days, his whereabouts were unknown. There was, of course, a great deal of speculation in the press. His spokesperson said that he was "hiking the Appalachian Trail," while questions were raised about who was acting as governor of South Carolina in his absence. When he reappeared, it turned out he had been on vacation in Buenos Aires with a woman who was not his wife. He was, of course, having an affair, which all came to light shortly after he came back from the trip. It also transpired that this wasn't the first time he had engaged in an extramarital affair. Due to both political and voter pressure, he had to resign.

This was also true in the case of the affair between former president Bill Clinton and Monica Lewinsky. In that story there was also ego involved, so two of the No-Os. However, the negative press didn't completely take him down, but this example of poor decision making severely affected his presidency and the country as a whole.

More recently, in 2021, Andrew Cuomo, the former governor of New York, resigned amid numerous sexual harassment allegations. Up until that news came to light, Governor Cuomo and his administration enjoyed numerous political successes during his tenure.

How many times have you seen a news story about a leader who has done something like send inappropriate photos to someone from their phone? Every time I see those stories, I see them as leadership failures.

MIKE'S LEADERSHIP LESSON: HANK AND RICK

Hank put his head in his hands as Charlotte turned on her heel and left the office, slamming the door behind her.

It didn't take long before Rick popped his head in. "I'm guessing Charlotte's not working her shift tomorrow?"

Hank sighed. "No, she quit," he said.

Rick shrugged. "Oh well, I think I know someone who might be able to fill in . . ." With that he left the office, and Hank thought, *here we go again!*

In the early years of the convenience store boom in the U.S., Hank and Rick saw an opportunity to run a really great business. Both of them were in college studying for their master's degrees. Hank was studying business and Rick was studying psychology.

From the early days, Hank focused on the business and how it was run behind the scenes. He looked after the money, inventory and all those aspects of the store. Rick, meanwhile, took care of hiring staff and dealing with customers.

However, gradually it became clear that Rick was hiring women that he liked and, over time, would start dating them. This made the dynamic among the staff strange and after a while there was a collective sigh of, "here we go again." Hank could always tell when things were starting to sour in the relationship, because the woman would be unusually quiet at work, or start phoning in sick for shifts here and there. Then, when the relationship ended, that woman would quit and the cycle would usually start again.

Hank tried to build up the courage to speak to Rick about it, but he always lost his nerve. He was introverted and hated conflict, and that made him reluctant to talk to Rick about his behavior.

He thought that if he himself behaved in an exemplary, professional way, that would help. So Hank tried to lead by example and make up for the damage Rick caused, but he was never able to balance everything out. Over time, Hank became resentful. He felt as though he put everything into the business, when all Rick did was take from it. Gradually, Hank and Rick's relationship became fractured and eventually their partnership broke down, which also saw the end of what had been a successful business and what could have been an incredible opportunity.

Leadership Lessons . . .

Many of us have worked in businesses with more than one manager, and what I learned very early on in my working life is that good leaders put in more than they take out of a business. On the face of it, Hank and Rick had complementary skills and knowledge with their respective backgrounds in business and psychology.

However, Rick used the business to serve himself, whereas Hank focused on the business and always tried to do the right thing. In the end, they were incompatible. Rick's leadership failures related to libido and although he may not have started out with the intention of basing his hiring decisions on whether he was attracted to the women applying, this became a pattern of behavior.

We tend to make mistakes in small steps and we also tend to accept dysfunction a little bit at a time. On a personal level, having awareness of the No-Os and being able to recognize their impact on your own leadership decisions can really help you to stay on the right track and alter your decisions to become a better leader. If you notice any one of the No-Os influencing your leadership decisions, know that it's never too late to change, but also that you have to change. Remember that Leaders Worth Following change themselves first.

Although it was Rick's behavior that caused the biggest issues at the convenience store, Hank wasn't helping this situation. Like many people, he wanted to avoid conflict and because he was afraid to speak up or hurt Rick's feelings, he didn't communicate his concerns or frustrations with Rick. Hank's leadership failure can also be seen in the light of a No-Os failure, albeit a very subtle one. Hank was worried about his image of being a nice and personable guy. His failure was one of ego, not about having an overly large ego, but an ego preoccupied with a seemingly helpful self-image. Hank's ego was overly protecting him from negative feelings associated with thinking that people woudn't see him as a personable and pleasant leader.

Remember that the only thing you can change is yourself. If you're part of a business partnership where you are giving and the other person is taking, start by looking at your approach to communication. Are you having open and honest conversations, or are you being passive-aggressive, dropping hints and becoming increasingly frustrated that nothing is changing?

If it's the latter, think about what you can do differently in terms of how you're communicating, because your hesitation to directly engage is part of the problem.

If you are having those frank conversations, however, and still nothing is changing, then you should probably leave that partnership. Accept that you are the only person that you can change in any situation, and sometimes that means walking away.

Don't allow your passions to rule your decisions and behavior as a leader. Equally, make sure you're not feeding into someone else's leadership failures by failing to take action yourself.

It's important to note that libido isn't restricted to its sexual context. It's also about how we use our power over other people. It can also refer to instances where someone is sucking power away from someone else.

If we look at the example of Donald Trump, and I'm not going to throw stones at him from a political perspective, I think you can see that all three No-Os—ego, dinero, and libido—are issues there, and when I look at that through a leadership lens, that's failed leadership.

When the three No-Os are unrestrained in how you lead, you cannot be effective. You may have short-term success, or you may have enough power and gravitas to lead for a time, but you won't find long-term leadership success.

LEAVING A LEGACY

Leadership, for me, is influencing people and ensuring that your time at the helm leaves a team, a department, or an organization better than how you found it. Your legacy doesn't have to be anything huge; it simply has to be that you left things better than you found them.

Being cognizant of the No-Os of leadership and checking your behavior, decision making, and thinking against them will make you a better leader: one who is easier to follow. Your people will have more loyalty and respect for you and, ultimately, your organization, or your team will perform better over time.

The No-Os of leadership aren't about casting judgments. They are there to guide you. When you're making decisions, decide what kind of leader you want to be. Nobody decides they want to be an egotistical leader. Nobody wants to be a leader so they can take financial advantage of others. Nobody wants to be a leader who takes advantage of people or who abuses their position of power.

As you go through life and encounter situations, be aware of ego, dinero, and libido as potential landmines that you, as a leader, can step on. When you're aware of these three landmines, you have a much better chance of navigating your leadership journey without setting them off.

This brings us full circle to self-awareness and taking the time to reflect so that you can understand situations and reactions. This gives you the time to self-regulate and side-step the landmines of the No-Os—there's a reason it's the first element on the road to becoming A Leader Worth Following.

These are three areas where I've seen many leaders fail. If you want to lead well over time and become A Leader Worth Following, you need to have respect for your people; and if you're not checking yourself on the No-Os, you won't have that respect for them and, as a consequence, they won't respect you.

CHAPTER 15

SELF-CARE FOR LEADERS

"You can't give to others what you have not given first to yourself."

Self-care is an important aspect of becoming A Leader Worth Following because, as leaders, we tend to spend our time taking care of everyone and everything but ourselves. The irony is that, on the face of it, the payback for working harder and longer can often feel pretty good—you feel as though you're getting more done at work; you may even receive more compensation as a result of doing so. However, if your aspiration, like mine, is to become A Leader Worth Following, it's important to remember that you can't give to others what you haven't first given to yourself.

If we look at the eight elements of being A Leader Worth Following, we can see that self-care ties into each of them. Being self-aware helps you understand your effect on your team and helps them to do their jobs better. Having empathy helps you better understand what it's like for other people to be around you, as well as understand where other people are coming from.

When you are willing to teach, you're open with people, you share and are generous with your knowledge, experience, and time. Having great expectations and an even greater heart really speaks to finding the balance between expecting a lot from your people but also understanding that on some days, just getting out of bed and into work might be a heroic act for someone. Facing reality means you can see things clearly and be genuine with those you lead and work with.

Owning your weaknesses and knowing when to ask for help encompasses the concept of vulnerability, which is essential for A Leader Worth Following. In fact, owning your weaknesses and being vulnerable is an essential part of being human, because if we can't recognize and take responsibility for our own weaknesses, we are more likely to push those onto others. When this happens, we move away from being a coach or mentor and shift into a place where we criticize others or jump in to rescue them too quickly, neither of which is the best place from which to operate.

Being mentally tough and emotionally predictable means you are resilient and your people know what to expect from you. Finding that resilience and emotional predictability is far easier when you look after yourself. Finally, changing yourself first means that you understand that all of us, yourself included, are a work in progress and that your journey towards becoming A Leader Worth Following is a journey and not a destination.

WHY IS SELF-CARE SO IMPORTANT FOR LEADERS?

If you find you are putting everything into your work, spending long hours and never stopping to look after yourself, you will likely be operating from a place of stress and depletion. Often as leaders we don't even realize we are operating in this mode until something bad happens.

The thing is, if we're not taking care of ourselves then things don't fall apart in just one day—if you miss your morning workout, everything won't crumble around you. But failing to take care of ourselves is like death by a thousand cuts. It builds up over time, and that's what is so insidious about a lack of self-care—often we don't realize how much we've been neglecting ourselves until that big event happens and lays bare everything we haven't been doing to look after ourselves.

If you look back at how you've been working, you may also notice that some of those eight pillars of being A Leader Worth Following have started to erode as you've let go of any good self-care habits you once had in place. This is why self-care is so integral to becoming A Leader Worth Following, because it underpins every one of those eight elements.

As I said at the beginning of this chapter, you can't give to others what you haven't given to yourself. When you're leading, whether a team or a whole organization, you'll spend a great deal of time meeting your team and employees, helping them with their struggles, making suggestions, and coaching them to overcome the obstacles in their path.

Imagine for a moment that you're doing all of this while feeling depleted. How will you behave when someone brings you a challenge? If you're honest, you know that when you feel depleted, you won't be operating effectively. Depending on how depleted your reserves are, you may even come across as unapproachable to those on your wider team.

You may think you hide it well, but believe me when I say that people will notice the underlying vibe you give off, and they'll spot the expression on your face when they knock on your door—that split second before you're able to put your professional "mask" on—when your look portrays annoyance rather than support. If people start feeling that energy from you regularly, they'll stop knocking on your door, and they'll stop talking to you and sharing their challenges with you. As a result, you're won't be able to work with them in a way that brings out their best, because you haven't brought your best to your interactions.

As leaders, self-care, therefore, has to be a priority. It wasn't until I started moving into the world of counseling that the deep importance of self-care properly resonated with me. When you're a counselor, you have to prioritize self-care because you're working very closely with people, and during a session, you need to be focused and present, with no distractions.

When I reflected back on my leadership experience through this lens, I believe that the times when I performed best as a leader were the ones when I was truly rested and had taken care of myself. This was when I brought my best self to work for the company, my team, our customers, and myself.

WHAT DOES SELF-CARE LOOK LIKE?

I know that self-care has become something of a buzzword in recent years, and I have found it's helpful to break it down into smaller components. The reality is that self-care will look a little bit different for everybody. So, rather than coming up with a list of activities you can do for self-care, I've found it's more beneficial to consider self-care in relation to six dimensions. When you are hitting each of these six every day, you'll have a robust self-care practice that won't only benefit you, but also your team, your organization, and your customers or members. What's more, each of these dimensions also supports the eight elements of becoming A Leader Worth Following.

The six dimensions of self-care are:

▸ Social

▸ Spiritual

▸ Physical

▸ Occupational

▸ Organizational

▸ Emotional

All of these dimensions are interconnected and, as I said, what each of these looks like will differ for each of us. It's also worth being aware that depending on your position, your leadership style, and even your stage of life, what you do under each of these dimensions of self-care can change too. So if you create a self-care practice now, be aware that it might change in the years ahead.

CHANGE YOURSELF FIRST

Changing yourself first is one of the crucial elements that supports you on your journey to becoming A Leader Worth Following, and it's just as applicable when we talk about self-care. As leaders, we obviously want our people to take good care of themselves and bring their best selves to work. When they do that, the workplace will become more productive and more cohesive, and we'll notice that they not only put extra effort into their work, but also that they enjoy it more.

As leaders, we tend to put in long days; when others see us doing this, it makes them afraid to go home. If we never take a vacation, our people will see this as a sign that they can't stop either. If we're on the phone and email all weekend and late at night, sending messages to our team, we're subconsciously sending the signal that we expect them to be working too. Therefore, if we want our people to focus on their self-care, we have to focus on our own self-care first.

There is a balance to strike here though, because sometimes there will be things that you just need to get out of your head at 10:00 p.m. on a Friday so you can relax for the weekend. Technology has made it easier than ever for us to work at all times of the day, but we can also use technology to our advantage.

Imagine there are ten things you need to get out of your head, because they're driving you crazy. It's 10:00 p.m. on a Friday. Examine the situation through the elements of being A Leader Worth Following. First, you've had the self-awareness to recognize that you need to get these things out of your head. Now you need to have empathy for the person or people who are going to receive your email at 10:00 p.m. on a Friday and think that's a call to action for them. Could you write and schedule the email to go out first thing Monday morning, instead of on Friday night? That way it's out of your head, and you're not inadvertently sending a signal to your people that you want them to work all weekend.

Of course, there will be times when you do need all hands on deck such as in an emergency situation that occurs late one evening or over a weekend. However, this should always be an exception, never the normal way of working.

If, like me, you want your people to take care of themselves, there is a much greater chance of that happening if you model this behavior for them. Lead by example and show them that when you're not at work, you're doing things to take care of yourself. I know this is easier said than done. So let's explore what that might look like under each of the six dimensions I've identified.

SOCIAL SELF-CARE

As humans, we're social creatures. We thrive when we're in relationships with others. As a leader you're continually mentoring people and helping them grow, but it's important that you have someone that you can go to, someone whom you connect with and to whom you are able to talk.

I'm sure you've heard the saying, "It's lonely at the top," and it does tend to be. This is why having people you connect with in every area of your life is important—you may have a social group at work, some close friends whom you either currently work with or previously worked with, as well as your personal friends and family. Maintaining those social connections with whoever falls into those categories is essential.

This doesn't mean you need to have long conversations with everyone in your social network each week or month. You can maintain those social connections with quick check-ins—a message saying, "Hey, just checking in, how are you doing?" is often enough.

You can extend this approach to your team, too, because doing so reminds them that you're there and shows that you care. It also feels good to have that connection, both for you and the person you're reaching out to.

SPIRITUAL SELF-CARE

This doesn't necessarily mean a religious practice, although it can be if that's what spirituality means to you. For me, the idea of spiritual self-care is to know that there is something bigger than all of us out there. In all honesty, anyone who thinks that they are the biggest thing in the universe likely has an issue with their ego, and these people who think of themselves first will struggle to find their path to becoming A Leader Worth Following.

When we come back to the idea that being A Leader Worth Following is all about service to others, it's easy to see how important it is to connect to something bigger than ourselves, whether that's a religion, being in nature, or other healing practices like meditation. Take some time to work out what it is that connects you to your higher power.

PHYSICAL SELF-CARE

Physical self-care is pretty obvious, in that it's taking care of our bodies. But I'd like to invite you to pause for a moment to think about what an incredible machine your body is. Think about everything it enables you to do, every single day. We all come into this world with a body, and we have the choice over whether we take care of it, or whether we abuse it.

Being very clear about what taking care of our bodies looks like is important, whether that's in the form of exercising, or thinking about what we eat or otherwise consume. Our diet is just one part of this picture; what else do we consume? For example, we all know alcohol and drugs are bad for our physical health, so what choices are we making around those? Physical self-care also means making sure we are well rested.

Being active and moving our bodies is also important, so when we are considering our self-care practice, we need to consider how to actively move each day as part of that. This might be a walk, a run, yoga, or even simply breathing with intention.

OCCUPATIONAL SELF-CARE

This is all about continuing to increase our competence in various areas of our lives, not only in a professional capacity. So, a CFO doesn't necessarily have to spend time improving their competence in financial matters. Maybe that CFO has a hobby like painting that they want to improve in. Or maybe there's another area of their role, like public speaking, that they want to get better at.

Perhaps you'd like to get better at public speaking too, or maybe you have a hobby, like playing music, learning a new language, or drawing. The important thing isn't where you grow your competence, but that you are doing so in areas that you enjoy both at work and in your personal life.

ORGANIZATIONAL SELF-CARE

This is one of my favorite dimensions of self-care. When I say organizational, I don't mean the organization you work for. Instead, I'm talking about keeping things organized, because many of us feel better when things are organized.

One great practice that was taught to me years ago was to simply straighten my desk before I finish for the day. If you've got piles of papers or files on your desk, even just straightening the piles can make them feel more ordered. Doing this at the end of each day feels therapeutic and helps you reset for the following day.

Organizational self-care can also encompass decluttering your office space, or it could be something simple like washing your car. A little bit of organization is important, but remember that it doesn't have to be a big action every time—sometimes just straightening the piles of papers is enough.

EMOTIONAL SELF-CARE

When you look at the eight elements of becoming A Leader Worth Following, you'll see that they all relate to emotions. Perhaps you are a leader who tells yourself you don't really need emotions—I know I thought that way for a long time until I realized that much better decisions could be made when I recognized their emotional component.

Emotions come as part of the package of what it is to be human—we're thinking creatures, but we're also emotional creatures, and denying your emotional side cuts out a big part of your ability to make decisions. In business, many of the complicated decisions we have to make as leaders aren't black and white; we spend a lot of our time in a gray area. Being emotionally present helps us have the capacity and resilience we need to make good assumptions and ultimately make good judgements.

In Chapter 8, I talked about how to let other people's energy (and emotions) wash over you, much like flowing with a big wave in the ocean, rather than trying to fight against it. Dealing with your own emotions is no different. Our emotions can feel like a big wave that's going to knock us off our feet, but if we can let those emotions in, even when they feel overwhelming for a time, we'll be better off once we're on the other side of them.

When you're in the ocean, the trick is to ride the wave; body surf along with it until it takes you into the shallows where you can stand. When you hit it just right, the wave's surge will catch you, propel you, and then set you down relatively gently as the wave runs out of power. If you try to fight against a wave, however, you'll often find yourself in underwater turbulence. You'll still move into shallower water, but you'll do so by being rolled around, hit by sand, and feeling completely disoriented. Panic might set in, but then all of a sudden you realize you're in only six inches of water, the wave has passed, and you can stand up and breathe again.

Emotions can be a lot like those waves. They can overwhelm you and make you feel like you're drowning, especially when you try to deny them or fight them. Or they can teach you a great deal when you relax into them and let them come. The thing is, just like the waves in the ocean, our emotions will keep coming whether we want them to or not. Being able to experience your emotions is not only important for your self-care, but also as a leader. When you can draw on your emotions, you can use them to help you reach decisions in complex situations that don't have a right or wrong answer.

Emotional self-care involves creating, strengthening, and maintaining our connections with those who are important to us, including ourselves. One of the best ways I've found to connect more helpfully with my emotions is to journal. Journaling is a useful tool for exploring what's going on within us and getting below the surface of our everyday interactions with ourselves and others. Connecting with our emotions is what creates connection and intimacy.

When we can recognize and identify our emotions, we can work out whether an emotion we're feeling is related to our present, or whether it's an emotion we've experienced in the past that is somehow recurring or coming back at us. What I find particularly interesting about emotions is that when we remember a moment, we re-experience it and all the emotions we felt at the time, whether those are traumatic or really enjoyable. Often the triggers for re-experiencing emotions can be quite subtle, so as leaders we need to be in a position to identify whether the emotion we're feeling is a current emotion, or one that's coming from our past. This can be difficult.

If we've had a bad experience in the past, we'll often attribute what happened then to what's happening in the present situation. This can make life hard for both us and our teams. However, when we take a moment, breathe deeply, and seek to understand the emotions we're feeling, we can bring ourselves back to the present and move forward. If we don't do this, we'll keep re-experiencing those past emotions until we learn the lesson they are trying to teach us.

DEVELOPING A SELF-CARE PRACTICE

I've found the key to maintaining your self-care is to make it a practice, rather than consider it a habit. When you begin to practice something, it becomes an intentional part of your life. The more you practice each action or activity, the more they will become part of who you are and the more they will become part of your nature over time.

If you know your self-care practice could do with some work (and let's be honest, I think that's true for most of us), I have a suggestion for how you can build all six dimensions of self-care into your week without it feeling overwhelming. It's a very simple process and takes just seven weeks.

In week one, pick just one of the self-care dimensions I've shared in this chapter and commit to doing something that fulfills that dimension every day for a week. In week two, pick a second dimension and stack that onto the daily action you chose in week one. Each week for six weeks, add another dimension to your self-care practice stack. By the time you reach week seven, you should find that you're hitting all six dimensions of a strong self-care practice each day.

Remember also that one action or activity may hit several, or even all six, of these self-care dimensions. Taking a nature walk with a friend might hit the social, spiritual, and physical self-care dimensions, for example. When you have awareness of each of these dimensions of self-care, you can look at how to bundle them where possible.

If you need a physical reminder, a simple technique is to take six sticky notes and write one of the dimensions of self-care on each. Put them to one side of your desk, and when you've completed an action or activity that covers one or more of them, move your sticky note to the other side of your desk.

Often these practices don't take extra time; they simply require us to be mindful in how we go about our days. When you're starting your self-care practice in week one, it can be helpful to think about the smallest and easiest step you can take to move you in the direction in which you want to travel. This is the best way to introduce lasting and meaningful change in your life, because a series of small, measured, and incremental steps will keep you moving in the right direction without feeling overwhelmed. Big steps can be more intimidating, and therefore more challenging, than lots of small steps—ultimately you cover the same ground in the long run, but lots of small steps give you more opportunities to make progress.

As I've said already, we have to model the change we want to see in our teams, so if one of your goals as a leader is to encourage your team to take better care of themselves, I would urge you to develop your own self-care practice. Change yourself first.

CONCLUSION

Perhaps when you picked up this book you were curious about leadership and were hoping for a few takeaways for how you might up your game and improve your leadership skills. While I think this book has good takeaways no matter where you might be in your leadership journey, there is much more here than takeaways. This book invites you to see transformational leadership as a process not only for you, but also for the people and organization you serve. The invitation to dig deep is ever present throughout this book and hopefully it will inspire you in your journey to become A Leader Worth Following.

The concepts are easy to understand, yet a bit elusive to implement. The model involving the concept of leading yourself, leading teams, and leading organizations is not a new idea, but approaching that with a focus on the eight elements of becoming A Leader Worth Following is.

As a reminder, Leaders Worth Following are self-aware, have empathy, are willing to teach, have great expectations and an even greater heart, face reality, own their weaknesses and know how to ask for help, are mentally tough and emotionally predictable, and change themselves first. There are many great leaders out there, and great leadership stories to go along with them. The best leaders, those that truly desire to serve, understand the power of knowing themselves first and then lead from a heart of service to others.

Giving instead of taking, serving instead of being served, and enriching others: these are the hallmarks of A Leader Worth Following. This is a lifelong journey, not one that you will complete, but therein lies the beauty—there is always something wonderful to discover around the next corner.

In addition to exploring the three levels of the leadership continuum—self-leadership, leading teams, and leading organizations—through the lens of the elements of becoming A Leader Worth Following and learning how this manifests at each stage in your career, you have (I hope) also learned some useful tools to support you on your journey.

As I said, I wish I'd known about techniques like motivational interviewing and active listening when I began my leadership journey. It took me a long time to recognize the true value of self-care—my hope is that by sharing these tools here, you will use them and see the benefits as you progress as a leader.

I also hope you use the No-Os of leadership to check your decision making and help develop your self-awareness. This is their purpose on your journey to becoming A Leader Worth Following. Be willing to learn, both from your own experiences and those of others, and you will find your progress smoother and often quicker.

Dig deep my friend, and the gold will find you.

If the concepts you have read about in this book have resonated on your leadership journey, and you would like to join the movement of Leaders Worth Following, please reach out to learn how I can help you further via http://www.aleaderworthfollowing.com. I offer executive coaching opportunities based on my experiences both in business and the world. With my master's degree in clinical mental health counseling, I'm ideally positioned to offer both life and executive coaching, as well as help you identify other areas of your life where you may be facing long-term issues and make referrals to other professionals who can support you.

From a leadership development perspective, the reason that this is so important is that you cannot separate your work self from your personal self, so you want to make each as strong as they can possibly be. This book, along with my fictional book *The Antics,* form a practice that offers life coaching in addition to executive coaching opportunities to help people in every area of their lives. Our work selves and our personal selves are not two distinct pieces; they have to work together and be integrated to allow us to lead more fulfilling lives.

Printed in the USA
CPSIA information can be obtained
at www.ICGtesting.com
JSHW080505240724
66866JS00001B/4